THE 1L GUIDE TO LEGAL WRITING

THE 1L GUIDE TO LEGAL WRITING

Kamina Pinder

Professor of Practice
Emory University School of Law

CAROLINA ACADEMIC PRESS
Durham, North Carolina

LIBRARY OF CONGRESS CATALOGING-IN-PUBLICATION DATA

Names: Pinder, Kamina, author.
Title: The 1L guide to legal writing / Kamina Pinder.
Description: Durham, North Carolina : Carolina Academic Press, 2024. | Includes bibliographical references and index.
Identifiers: LCCN 2024006493 | ISBN 9781531020545 (paperback) | ISBN 9781531020552 (ebook)
Subjects: LCSH: Legal composition. | Law—United States—Language.
Classification: LCC KF250 .P56 2024 | DDC 808.06/634—dc23/eng/20240214
LC record available at https://lccn.loc.gov/2024006493

CAROLINA ACADEMIC PRESS
700 Kent Street
Durham, North Carolina 27701
(919) 489-7486
www.cap-press.com

PRINTED IN THE UNITED STATES OF AMERICA

Contents

PART II PERSUASIVE WRITING
(a.k.a. the Appellate Brief or Motion)

PART III WRITING BEYOND THE CLASSROOM

Acknowledgments

This book is dedicated to my parents, Frank and Lover Henderson; my daughter, Spencer Jack; and my sister, Karen Mitchell.

Special thank you for the invaluable contributions and edits of my research assistants: Charli Davis, Mackenzie Ward, Suresh Boodram, Nora Maloney, Beth Petras, and Isabella Ryan.

And I am grateful for the support and general feedback of my legal writing colleagues at Emory University School of Law, and of students Constance Couch, Lexie Carmon, Laney Foeller, Robert Schmidt, Audrey Smith-Roetto, and Michelle Podolnyy.

And finally, I thank Ally Templin and Hilarie Gaylin for their inspiration and encouragement, respectively.

Preface

Why I Wrote This Book

Dear 1L,

I am beginning this book with a confession. I always swore I would not write a book on legal writing. There are plenty of legal writing books out there, and I was not sure I had anything new to add on the topic. Then I realized that my students rarely did much reading of any writing book I assigned to the class. I did not reference the books very frequently, and to the extent I did it was frequently to make distinctions. I recognize that the casebook readings for doctrinal courses are already overwhelming (I also teach Contracts, so I know firsthand how much reading you have), and that if there is reading that 1L students are going to give short shrift, it will be the reading for the legal writing class. Also, the workload of legal writing classes typically outweighs the number of credits the students earn for the class. Accordingly, I wrote this book to provide students a no-frills, straightforward reference for legal writing concepts.

I tell my students that teaching legal writing is a lot like teaching someone to drive. I can talk about driving until I am blue in the face: telling you where to put your hands on the wheel, how to adjust your mirrors, and what to do with the gas pedal, gears, brakes, traffic rules, etcetera; but most of your learning will occur when you actually do it yourself. Similarly, most of your learning about legal writing will come from actually applying what your professor teaches you, and then through your individual conferences with your professor and your ongoing editorial process. This book puts that learning in a framework by providing guidance followed by clear examples.

The book is organized in three parts. The first two parts parallel the typical structure of a 1L legal writing program. Part I addresses the predictive memorandum of the first semester, and Part II illustrates how to write persuasively through the common second-semester paradigm of the appellate brief. Part III includes a number of resources and examples that are meant to complement the reading and assist you in writing that extends beyond your classroom assignments.

For the sake of simplicity and consistency, all the examples in this book stem from the same fact pattern. This fact pattern, which follows this preface, is a promissory estoppel (think Contracts) issue about a law student to whom a law firm promised future employment and later reneged.

What This Book Is Not

This book will not teach you how to research, cite, or select cases that you will use in legal documents. Your legal writing professor, law librarian, or someone else will teach you that. I promised you the basics, and that would go beyond the basics. I recognize that even if your attention span were unlimited, I am competing for your time and attention with reading from doctrinal casebooks, and perhaps even another legal writing book.

Most important, this is not a substitute for what you learn in your legal writing class. Of course, there is always some subjectivity involved in how professors approach legal writing, so to the extent that what you read differs from what your professor teaches you, by all means adopt the approach of the person who will grade your assignment.

Although it has been quite a long time, my memories of the feelings of excitement and anxiety of the first year of law school remain vivid. I hope that this book serves as a valuable resource as you take this auspicious journey.

Sincerely,
Professor Pinder

The Fact Pattern

The following is a brief summary of the fact pattern on which all examples in this book are based. Law student writers Charli Davis and Mackenzie Ward drafted the memorandum and appellate briefs; their writing focused on the reliance and detriment elements of promissory estoppel.

> A New Jersey top-ranked law firm hired a first-year law student for its summer program. The student provided very impressive work over the summer; consequently, even though it was the midst of an economic recession, the firm offered him a job after he graduated conditioned on his continued strong performance in law school.
>
> Comfortable in the knowledge that he had a job awaiting him after graduation, the law student relaxed his academic performance in law school, though he did remain on the Dean's List. The student continued to work for the law firm his second summer and during his third year—forgoing interviewing at other law firms, externship opportunities, and a potential spot on the executive board of the law school's main law journal.
>
> When the economy did not recover, the firm notified the student during his third year of law school that it would not hire him after graduation. The student obtained a job as an associate with a solo practitioner in Delaware at approximately twenty-five percent of the starting salary that the law firm would have paid.

THE 1L GUIDE TO LEGAL WRITING

PART I

Predictive Writing

(a.k.a. the Memorandum)

ONE

The Big Picture

This chapter introduces the reader to predictive and objective writing through a discussion of the purpose and likely context of a legal memorandum. It notes that predictive means making predictions in the context of summary judgment, not in terms of what a judge or jury is likely to conclude. This chapter introduces the reader to the oft-applied acronyms in the legal writing class. It explains the significance of the acronyms and how they help organize legal writing in a logical fashion; it also explains why I chose to adopt the CREACC acronym.

TWO

Questions (or Issues) Presented

This chapter discusses substantively what should be included in an Issues Presented section. It also includes a couple of different ways to effectively write the section.

THREE

Brief Answers

This chapter discusses the format and substance of a Brief Answers section.

FOUR

Statement of Facts

This relatively short chapter includes general tips and an explanation for why, after completing the memorandum, the Statement of Facts is the section that the writer should edit last.

FIVE

Macro-Organization: Issues and Sub-Issues

This chapter introduces the concept of the roadmap—also known as the umbrella—section of the memorandum. It details how to use the memorandum problem and the applicable rules of law to discern the relevant issues and dispose of those that are not at issue.

SIX

Conclusion

This chapter briefly explains and illustrates the conclusion section of a memorandum.

SEVEN

Rule

This chapter illustrates how to identify and synthesize a Rule where appropriate.

EIGHT

Rule Explanation

This chapter describes rule Explanation with a special emphasis on how to "organize by premise" rather than by case, and how to organize treatment of both authority and counter-authority.

NINE

Analysis

This chapter emphasizes the importance of Analysis in legal writing. It discusses analytical organization through the concept of "organizing by assertion," and through example demonstrates what commonly strengthens and weakens analytical comparisons.

TEN

Counter-Analysis

Counter-Analysis is inherently part of Analysis. However, I now include it in my legal writing acronym as a separate "letter" because it is otherwise frequently overlooked by students. Accordingly, I dedicate a chapter to Counter-Analysis that discusses its importance as part of Analysis; I also include examples of effective and ineffective Counter-Analysis.

ONE

The Big Picture

The style of writing in memoranda is often described as objective or predictive. Both descriptions are accurate; the memorandum will predict the strength and weakness of a legal position, but the writer has no stake in the outcome, so the style is objective. Some times students feel the need to support the client's position, even if that position is not a legally tenable one. Do not make this mistake. The memorandum can be used for a number of purposes, and if you do not write it objectively, you may undermine its purpose. For example, your supervisor may use the memorandum to develop a legal strategy or in deciding whether to take the client's case. Before developing a legal strategy, the reader needs to fully understand the implications of the law on the situation.

When you write anything, your primary consideration should always be your audience. With respect to a legal memorandum, that audience will be a legal supervisor and, occasionally, the client. Of course, your legal writing professor is likely the reader of your first legal memorandum. Whoever the reader, the writing must be clear. In an industry where time is of the essence, your memorandum should be written for a deep read or a cursory

> **PROF'S TIPS**
> Part of writing clearly includes writing in active voice. Do not write in passive voice unless there is a compelling reason to do so. For more about active and passive voice, see Chapter 17.

glance. The reader should be able to look at any heading and know exactly what to expect. In the 1993 Oscar-winning movie *Philadelphia*, Denzel Washington's lawyer character repeatedly says, "Explain this to me like I'm a two-year-old." You are certainly not writing for a toddler, but pretend there is one on your shoulder constantly asking "WHY?" Much of your effectiveness as a legal writer is based on your ability to support your assertions. If you cannot explain the "whys," your writing is less credible.

Understanding your audience requires that you understand the purpose of the document you are writing. In the litigation process, the legal memorandum is an early document (see step 4 in the litigation timeline in the following section). In your legal writing class, it is more likely that you will write a memorandum on a civil issue rather than a criminal one, so your framework is composed around issues of civil liability rather than criminal culpability or guilt. After reviewing the facts of the claim, the memorandum evaluates its viability. The writer's task is to evaluate whether, on the basis of legal research, the plaintiff has a viable legal claim. Viability does not speak to what a judge or jury will ultimately hold, but whether the claim is likely to survive summary judgment (for a more in-depth description of summary judgment, see Chapter 18). In other words, the memorandum seeks to determine whether the plaintiff can support a prima facie case.

FEDERAL CIVIL LITIGATION TIMELINE

1. Event giving rise to claim
2. Client interview and necessary additional factual research
3. Legal research
4. **OFFICE MEMORANDUM** ← **YOU ARE HERE**
5. Client letter and decision whether to pursue claim
6. File and serve complaint

7 Answer to complaint

8 Discovery

9 Arbitration (possibly)

10 Pre-trial motions

11 Possible settlement

12 Trial

13 Verdict by jury or judgment by court

14 Possible notice of appeal

15 Appellant and appellee submit briefs specified in scheduling order

16 Screening for oral argument by staff attorneys at the court of appeals

17 Oral argument

18 Panel of court of appeals deliberates and issues opinion and order

19 Either party may petition for a rehearing on *en banc* (heard by all the judges on the particular court)

20 *En banc* court of appeals may review brief and hear oral argument

21 *En banc* court of appeals issues opinion and order

22 Either party may appeal to the U.S. Supreme Court

23 Parties submit briefs and argue before the Court

24 The Court issues opinion and order

What's in an Acronym?

Early in the first semester, I tell my students that the key to success in law school is largely dependent on their ability to do three things: issue spot, organize, and (especially) analyze. This is true for both legal writing and doctrinal classes. Sounds simple, right? It is not, but working within a framework certainly makes writing this way conceptually easier.

One of the first concepts to which your legal writing professor will introduce you is his or her acronym of choice. While you are unlikely to hear your future legal supervisor refer to an acronym, good legal writers all follow the same common structure for legal documents. And you will learn, law students love acronyms as mnemonic devices. The time-tested acronym for exam writing is IRAC—Issue, Rule, Analysis, and Conclusion. A few legal writing professors implement IRAC for their class, but most will use some variation of the following: REAC (Rule, rule Explanation, Analysis, and Conclusion), TR-EAC (Thesis, Rule, rule Explanation, Analysis, and Conclusion), or CRAC (Conclusion, Rule, rule Analysis, and Conclusion). My preference, and the acronym I will reference throughout the majority of the book, is CREACC (Conclusion, Rule, rule Explanation, Analysis, Counter-Analysis, and Conclusion).

> **PROF'S TIPS**
> Note that I capitalize the first letter of each of the elements of the acronym; I do that for emphasis throughout the book. You would not be expected to do the same.

> **PROF'S TIPS**
> CREACCs can vary in length, from a paragraph to pages.

Legal writing is logical. Accordingly, irrespective of acronym, legal writing requires the same basic structure. For any legal issue begin with your legal position: your conclusion. Then provide the rule(s) that support that legal conclusion. Before you can predict how those rules will apply to the legal situation you are confronting, you must first explain and illustrate how courts (preferably in your jurisdiction) have applied those rules. This is reminiscent of the adage, "Say what you are going to say, say it, and then say what you have said."

Consistent with this model, for every issue you analyze there will be a CREACC. I often tell students to think of what you are writing as a mathematical proof; even if you have the right answer, you will not receive credit unless you show your work. Using an acronym provides a formula through which you can support your legal conclusion; the conclusion you draw is typically less important to your professor than your ability to support it. The next several chapters will detail how to organize the information and the general substance to include.

END OF CHAPTER SUMMARY

- Understand the task you were assigned.
- Write for your audience.
- Adopt an organizational structure for your document.

TWO

Questions (or Issues) Presented

The Question(s) Presented section sets forth the legal issues that the memorandum will resolve. It is a helpful resource for readers who may want to learn quickly whether the memorandum is useful to them. Renowned legal writing scholar Bryan Garner, in his article *The Deep Issue: A New Approach to Framing Legal Issues*, provides that the Question(s) Presented should be no longer than seventy-five words per question, and while that is not a mandate, it is a good guideline. There can be a question for each issue the memorandum addresses, or, as the example below illustrates, there can be a question presented that includes a broad topic—in this case, promissory estoppel—that encompasses the sub-issues that will be CREACCs—reasonable reliance and detriment.

There are two common ways to write a Question(s) Presented section. The first, and most conventional, is to write the question as a single sentence that includes the legal issue and its factual basis. Alternatively, if the fact pattern is so complex that it is difficult to capture it in a single sentence, you can write a short paragraph that summarizes the legally relevant facts (i.e., facts necessary or helpful in actually answering the question), and then write a question or questions that include only the legal questions.

> **PROF'S TIPS**
> Your professor is likely to require you to write the question presented as a single sentence, so if you are tempted to write a question presented in the style of "Type 2," ask your professor first.

Below are examples of a question from a Question(s) Presented section. The first, categorized below as Type 1, includes the question as a single sentence (the first is a question framed with a question mark, while the second is a single-sentence question that begins with the word "whether" and does not include a question mark). Your professor may express a preference of one format over another. The second, categorized as Type 2, is the paragraph of facts followed by the question that encapsulates a legal conclusion in a single sentence.

Type 1 (Single-Sentence Question)

Question with a Question Mark

1. Under New Jersey law, can recent law school graduate Mr. Spencer Li support a case of promissory estoppel against Micheo & Yoon by establishing that his reliance on the law firm's promise of post-graduation employment made the summer after Mr. Li's first year was reasonable, and that this reliance resulted in definite and substantial detriment to Mr. Li?

Question as a Statement

1. Whether under New Jersey law, recent law school graduate Spencer Li can support a case of promissory estoppel against Micheo & Yoon, by establishing that his reliance on the law firm's promise of post-law school graduation employment made the summer after Mr. Li's first year of law school was reasonable, and that this reliance resulted in definite and substantial detriment to Mr. Li.

Type 2 (Fact Paragraph Followed by the Legal Question or Questions)

At the completion of his summer associate position after his first year of law school, the Director of Attorney Recruiting at the law firm Micheo & Yoon offered law student, Mr. Spencer Li, a permanent job after graduation subject to his law school performance. Mr. Li's grade point average dropped, but he maintained a position on the law school's Dean's List; Mr. Li forwent opportunities to seek other law firm employment. The firm ultimately did not hire Mr. Li after he graduated because of an economic recession.

1. Can Mr. Li establish the reasonable reliance and detriment elements necessary to support a prima facie claim of promissory estoppel in New Jersey?

END OF CHAPTER SUMMARY

- The Question(s) or Issue(s) Presented section sets forth the legal issues.
- The number of questions in this section corresponds to the number of CREACCs in the memorandum.
- The question can either be written as a single sentence that includes the legal question and its factual basis or as a factual paragraph followed by the legal question(s).

THREE

Brief Answers

For every question in the Question(s) Presented section of a memorandum, there must be an answer in the Brief Answer(s) section. The Brief Answer provides the reader with a nutshell version of the legal conclusion and its factual basis. When you are writing your memorandum, you are writing it not only to answer a current legal issue, but also so that it may help answer similar legal questions in the future. Accordingly, the Question(s) Presented and the Brief Answer(s) combined should serve to quickly provide your reader with enough information to determine whether she needs to read further.

> **PROF'S TIPS**
> In describing the facts of the situation, use not just the party names, but also the generic role or description.

A Brief Answer typically begins with a sentence comprised of a one- or two-word answer to the question: yes, no, probably yes, probably no. That sentence is followed by the applicable rule, with no citation, followed by a summary of its application to the facts. Remember, the Brief Answer should be brief—ideally it should be no longer than a paragraph. Depending on the complexity of the rule, the paragraph may be a slightly longer one, and rarely does it span multiple paragraphs.

1. No. In New Jersey, a prima facie claim for promissory estoppel requires, *inter alia*, the promisee to reasonably rely on the promise and then incur a definite and substantial detriment based on that reliance. While Mr. Li did rely on the firm's promise, it was not reasonable to do so because the promise was for employment too far in the future, Mr. Li let his grades fall, and there was an economic recession at the time of the promise. Moreover, there was no definite detriment because Mr. Li's allegation of damage is not calculable; nor was there a substantial detriment because Mr. Li still gained valuable experience from working with the firm and he was not prevented from seeking employment elsewhere.

PROF'S TIPS

Note that the writer begins with a rule statement followed by a summary of the facts as they apply to that rule.

END OF CHAPTER SUMMARY

- Brief Answer(s) is a paragraph that includes a short-sentence answer of one or two words. It is then followed by a rule statement for the issue and a brief application of that rule.
- There is no citation in the Brief Answer(s).

FOUR

Statement of Facts

A Statement of Facts in a memorandum is a summary of the legally relevant facts in a context that makes them understandable. The Statement of Facts is written with an objective tone, and as with all your writing, the writing should be clear and easy to read.

When I grade a Statement of Facts for a memorandum, I first look at the quality of writing; unsurprisingly, law students are typically able to write a good summary of the important facts. So how then do I make distinctions among quality? The easiest way to grade student work is to read the Statement of Facts last, after I have read the Analysis section. Why? The Analysis section is the only part of the CREACC that includes facts from the legal situation. If there are facts important enough to include in the analysis, then those facts should also be in the Statement of Facts. If the student includes facts in the discussion that were not included in the Statement of Facts, I lower the grade. Accordingly, while you may draft your Statement of Facts early, you should always review and edit it after you finish writing your Analysis section.

> **PROF'S TIPS**
>
> Legally relevant facts are those facts necessary to effectively analyze the legal issue.

END OF CHAPTER SUMMARY

- The Statement of Facts is typically a clear chronological summary of the legally relevant facts of the situation.
- Write in clear prose.
- There should not be facts in your Analysis that do not appear in the Statement of Facts.
- Draft the Statement of Facts early, but finalize it after completing the rest of your memorandum.

FIVE

Macro-Organization: Issues and Sub-Issues

Once you have identified the legal issue(s) and understand through research the legal rules that govern the law at issue (see Chapter 8), there needs to be a place in the memorandum to put them in context for the reader. That place is the roadmap. The roadmap—sometimes called the umbrella—is the introduction and overview to the legal issues the memorandum will address. Before the CREACC or CREACCs, a roadmap puts the ensuing discussion in context; it explains why the writer is addressing the issues and, if appropriate, how those issues relate to each other.

> **PROF'S TIPS**
> Note that the general organization throughout a memorandum is like a funnel—from broad to specific.

A roadmap can provide context in various ways. A roadmap for a single issue provides enough context for the reader to understand why that issue should be important to the reader. It may include brief factual background, or even the background for the law at issue, including purpose of the law or policy. A roadmap for multiple issues may incorporate the same content as a single-issue roadmap, but it also finds a way to describe to the reader how the multiple issues are connected; it is also where the writer eliminates elements of a rule that are not at issue. Below are examples of a single-issue and a multiple-issue roadmap.

Single-Issue Roadmap

The following is a roadmap if reasonable reliance were the only issue to address under promissory estoppel. It includes the purpose of the memorandum, the macro-rule, and how the writers turned their focus specifically to reasonable reliance.

PROF'S TIPS
This is the factual basis of the claim.

PROF'S TIPS
This section provides context by setting forth the purpose of the rule.

PROF'S TIPS
This is the macro- or overarching rule.

DISCUSSION

Spencer Li is bringing a promissory estoppel claim against his former employer, Micheo & Yoon, for reneging on its promise to hire him full-time after he graduated from law school. Promissory estoppel is a remedy by which a promisee may seek redress when a promisor should reasonably expect his promise to induce forbearance or action on the part of the promisee, limited to when injustice can only be avoided by the enforcement of the promise. RESTATEMENT (SECOND) OF CONTRACTS § 139(1) (Am. Law Inst. 1981). Promissory estoppel is applicable to *in futuro* promises where the promisor intends to abandon the promise, or where the promise is intended to influence another into action or forbearance of a legal right. *See Friedman v. Tappan Dev. Corp.*, 126 A.2d 646, 653 (N.J. 1956).

In New Jersey, promissory estoppel requires: (1) the promisor made a definite promise; (2) the promisor made the promise expecting it to induce reliance by the promisee; (3) the promisee in fact reasonably relied on the promise; and (4) the promisee suffered a definite and substantial detriment because of reliance on the promise. *Malaker Corp. Stockholders Protective Comm. v. First Jersey Nat'l Bank*, 395 A.2d 222, 230 (N.J. Super. Ct. App. Div. 1978). The *sine qua non* for the applicability of promissory estoppel is the threshold element of a clear and definite promise. *Id.* at 230. Janet Heinan, the Director of Attorney Recruiting at Micheo & Yoon, told Mr. Li he would receive an offer from the firm if he met certain conditions, so there was a definite promise. That the Director of Attorney Recruiting made the promise and gave certain conditions to its fulfillment implies that Mr. Li was expected to rely on the promise. Another associate is researching the issue of detrimental reliance. Therefore, at issue in this memorandum is whether Mr. Li reasonably relied on this promise.

PROF'S TIPS
The roadmap eliminated elements not at issue and identified the remaining issues it will address.

Even though Mr. Li did rely on the law firm's promise, his reliance was not reasonable because: he failed to meet certain conditions of the promise, the time between when the promise was made and its expected performance was too long, and there were economic factors beyond the promisor's control. To satisfy the third element of a claim for promissory estoppel, a plaintiff must show that he reasonably relied on a representation made by the defendant, which induced him to abandon an existing right or influenced him to act or refrain from acting. *Friedman*, 126 A.2d at 653.

PROF'S TIPS
This is the first sentence of the CREACC; it is the conclusion sentence. It could also be a point heading.

PROF'S TIPS
This is the rule for the reliance CREACCC.

Multi-Issue Roadmap with an Overarching Rule

If there is an overarching rule comprised of multiple elements or factors that govern the issues, that rule is called the macro-rule. For example, in the sample memorandum in this book, the macro-rule is the rule for promissory estoppel. In the memorandum, as per their instructions, the writers only addressed two of the four elements of promissory estoppel. The roadmap allowed the writers to set out promissory estoppel as the macro-rule, dispose of the non-determinative elements, and explain why those elements are not at issue. The following is a multi-issue roadmap for promissory estoppel.

DISCUSSION

I. Mr. Li cannot support a prima facie claim of promissory estoppel against the law firm because, although the law firm made a definite promise with an expectation Mr. Li would rely on that promise, his reliance on that promise was not reasonable, and his detriment was neither definite nor substantial.

> **PROF'S TIPS**
> This major heading summarizes both claims at issue; the subheadings will specifically address the claim in the CREACCs to follow. While headings are important organizational tools in a memorandum, point headings are not a necessity; please see Chapter 15 for further explanation of point headings. A regular heading for this section could simply read **Promissory Estoppel**, while a subheading could be **Reliance Damages**.

> **PROF'S TIPS**
> A statement summarizing the basic claim.

> **PROF'S TIPS**
> Notice that the writers are only examining the strength of the claim; they do not write what a judge or jury will decide or hold.

> **PROF'S TIPS**
> This is the contextual background—in this case, the purpose of the law and its applicability.

Spencer Li is bringing a promissory estoppel claim against his former employer, Micheo & Yoon, for reneging on its promise to hire him full-time after he graduated from law school. Promissory estoppel is a remedy by which a promisee may seek redress when a promisor should reasonably expect his promise to induce forbearance or action on the part of the promisee, limited to when injustice can only be avoided by the enforcement of the promise. RESTATEMENT (SECOND) OF CONTRACTS § 139(1) (Am. Law Inst. 1981). Promissory estoppel is applicable to *in futuro* promises where the promisor intends to abandon the promise, or where the promise is intended to influence another into action or forbearance of a legal right. *See Friedman v. Tappan Dev. Corp.*, 126 A.2d 646, 653 (N.J. 1956).

In New Jersey, promissory estoppel requires: (1) the promisor made a definite promise; (2) the promisor made the promise expecting it to induce reliance by the promisee; (3) the promisee in fact reasonably relied on the promise; and (4) the promisee suffered a definite and substantial detriment because of reliance on the promise. *Malaker Corp. Stockholders Protective Comm. v. First Jersey Nat'l Bank*, 395 A.2d 222, 230 (N.J. Super. Ct. App. Div. 1978). The *sine qua non* for the applicability of promissory estoppel is the threshold element of a clear and definite promise. *Id.* at 230. Janet Heinan, the Director of Attorney Recruiting at Micheo & Yoon, told Mr. Li he would receive an offer from the firm if he met certain conditions, so there was a definite promise. That the Director of Attorney Recruiting made the promise and gave certain conditions to its fulfillment implies that Mr. Li was expected to rely on the promise. Therefore, at issue here is whether Mr. Li reasonably relied on this promise, and if so, whether this reliance forced Mr. Li to incur a definite and substantial detriment.

PROF'S TIPS

This is the overarching (macro-) rule.

PROF'S TIPS

The roadmap eliminated elements not at issue and identified the remaining issues it will address.

A. **Even though Mr. Li did rely on the law firm's promise, his reliance was not reasonable because: he failed to meet certain conditions of the promise, the time between when the promise was made and its expected performance was too long, and there were economic factors beyond the promisor's control.**

PROF'S TIPS

This point heading is the single-sentence conclusion for the reasonable reliance CREACC. If you are not using point headings, that sentence is simply the Conclusion for the CREACC to follow.

Multi-Issue Roadmap with Distinct Legal Issues

Of course, not all multi-issue memoranda include multiple issues that fall under a single rule of law. The following is an example of a roadmap that addresses two separate but related rules of law.

DISCUSSION

PROF'S TIPS
This is the summary of the claim.

Spencer Li is bringing a breach of contract, and in the alternative promissory estoppel, claim against his former employer, Micheo & Yoon, for reneging on its promise to hire him full-time after he graduated from law school. This memorandum will first address the viability of Mr. Li's breach of contract claim, and then address the claim for promissory estoppel.

PROF'S TIPS
The writer identified the legal issues.

PROF'S TIPS
You can combine breach of contract and promissory estoppel into one heading and then use subheadings for each issue.

I. Mr. Li will not succeed on a breach of contract action because the oral promise to employ him after his law school graduation is precluded from enforcement by the Statute of Frauds.

[Roadmap for breach of contract, followed by discussion, goes here. If there are no sub-issues, there is no need for subheadings.]

PROF'S TIPS
Notice that the writer is only examining the strength of the claim; she does not write what a judge or jury will decide or hold.

II. Mr. Li cannot support a prima facie claim of promissory estoppel against the law firm because, although the law firm made a definite promise with an expectation Mr. Li would rely on that promise, his reliance on that promise was not reasonable, and his detriment was neither definite nor substantial.

Promissory estoppel is a remedy by which a promisee may seek redress when a promisor should reasonably expect his promise to induce forbearance or action on the part of the promisee, limited to when injustice can only be avoided by the enforcement of the promise. RESTATEMENT (SECOND) OF CONTRACTS § 139(1) (Am. Law Inst. 1981). Promissory estoppel is applicable to *in futuro* promises where the promisor intends to abandon the promise, or where the promise is intended to influence another into action or forbearance of a legal right. *See Friedman v. Tappan Dev. Corp.*, 126 A.2d 646, 653 (N.J. 1956).

In New Jersey, promissory estoppel requires: (1) the promisor made a definite promise; (2) the promisor made the promise expecting it to induce reliance by the promisee; (3) the promisee in fact reasonably relied on the promise; and (4) the promisee suffered a definite and substantial detriment because of reliance on the promise. *Malaker Corp. Stockholders Protective Comm. v. First Jersey Nat'l Bank*, 395 A.2d 222, 230 (N.J. Super. Ct. App. Div. 1978). The *sine qua non* for the applicability of promissory estoppel is the threshold element of a clear and definite promise. *Id.* at 230. Janet Heinan, the Director of Attorney Recruiting at Micheo & Yoon, told Mr. Li he would receive an offer from the firm if he met certain conditions, so there was a definite promise. That the Director of Attorney Recruiting made the promise and gave certain conditions to its fulfillment implies that Mr. Li was expected to rely on the promise. Therefore, at issue is whether Mr. Li reasonably relied on this promise, and if so, whether this reliance forced Mr. Li to incur a definite and substantial detriment.

A. **Even though Mr. Li did rely on the law firm's promise, his reliance was not reasonable because: he failed to meet certain conditions of the promise, the time between when the promise was made and its expected performance was too long, and there were economic factors beyond the promisor's control.**

PROF'S TIPS

Again, if you are not using point headings, this sentence is the Conclusion for the CREACC.

END OF CHAPTER SUMMARY

- Outline the legal issues.
- Separate the overarching issues and sub-issues.
- Use a roadmap to put the issues in context and to eliminate topics that may be in the law, but are not at issue in the memorandum.

SIX

Conclusion

The conclusion for a CREACC is typically a single-sentence summary of the writer's legal conclusion that appears at the beginning and end of the discussion of the issue. It answers the legal question and provides the basis.

If you are using point headings, that first C Conclusion is the point heading (for more instruction on how to write a point heading, see Chapter 15). If you are using headings that are not point headings, then the Conclusion follows the heading. A Conclusion does not merely identify the issue. Instead, it succinctly provides a legal position and its basis.

PROF'S TIPS

Note that this chapter is about Conclusions for CREACCS. The formal memorandum also includes a Conclusion section that summarizes the micro-conclusions for the memorandum, or, for a single-issue memorandum, rephrases and reiterates the CREACC conclusion.

The following is an example of the reasonable reliance Conclusion at the beginning of the reasonable reliance CREACC. In this book's memorandum, it is framed as a point heading, but it can also be the sentence following a heading that is not a point heading.

> Even though Mr. Li did rely on the law firm's promise, his reliance was not reasonable because: he failed to meet certain conditions of the promise, the time between when the promise was made and its expected performance was too long, and there were economic factors beyond the promisor's control.

Write a single-sentence Conclusion at the end of each CREACC. Because there is a Conclusion at the beginning and end of each CREACC, the content will be similar. The following is an example of the Conclusion at the end of the reasonable reliance CREACC.

PROF'S TIPS

Look for the word "because" or its equivalent as confirmation that you have included the basis of your position as part of the Conclusion.

> Because Mr. Li may not have met the conditions of the promise, was offered employment two years before he could take the position, and there were negative economic factors beyond the law firm's control impacting its ability to hire Mr. Li, it was not reasonable for Mr. Li to rely on Ms. Heinan's promise of employment.

There is also a formal Conclusion at the end of the memorandum that ties together all micro-conclusions. This Conclusion tends to be multiple sentences, but no more than a short paragraph.

> **CONCLUSION**
>
> Under New Jersey law, Mr. Li will have difficulty establishing a prima facie claim of promissory estoppel as he did not reasonably rely on Micheo & Yoon's promise to employ him after he graduated because the promise was made too remote in time from when it could be fulfilled. It is possible Mr. Li did not meet the conditions of the promise, and external economic pressures affected the law firm's ability to fulfill its promise to Mr. Li. Moreover, Mr. Li cannot establish the essential factors of a definite and substantial detriment because Mr. Li's lost potential earnings are mere speculation, and it was his choice to forgo other employment prospects.

END OF CHAPTER SUMMARY

- The Conclusion in the beginning of a CREACC is typically short. It includes the legal conclusion and a brief basis.
- Sometimes the Conclusion is a point-heading—a single-sentence Conclusion; if you are using point headings, in a multi-issue memorandum there is a broad point heading that addresses all of the legal issues, followed by your roadmap. There are then more specific point headings for each of the issues you will CREACC. Typically, you can follow the point heading for a CREACC with your rule, which is the next part of the CREACC.
- A macro-Conclusion summarizes all or several of the conclusions for the sub-issues. It appears in its own section at the end of the document.

SEVEN

Rule

After setting out the CREACC Conclusion—either as a point heading or a sentence—the writer must identify a rule of law that governs the discussion that ensues. If there is a macro-rule of law that governs the legal issue, it likely belongs in the roadmap section of your memorandum (see Chapter 5). This chapter specifically addresses the Rule statement for a CREACC.

Because the CREACC structure is designed to predict a legal outcome, the first step in creating the CREACC structure is to identify the governing rule. The governing rule can be as simple as a definition in the language of a statute or common law.

PROF'S TIPS

You can select a case for a clear Rule statement even if you do not intend to use its facts for case illustration.

Statutory Example

Sometimes the Rule statement comes from a statute, ordinance, or other source rather than common law (law derived from judicial decisions). If that is the case, then the Rule could be short and would likely be immediately followed by rule Explanation, perhaps even in the same paragraph (see example below). The promissory estoppel example on which this book relies is set in New Jersey, which does not have an applicable statute. However, Georgia is one of a minority of states with a promissory estoppel statute. This is what a roadmap of promissory estoppel followed by a CREACC of reasonable reliance may look like if the broad rule of law were based on a statute rather than common law.

> In Georgia, promissory estoppel is defined as "a promise which the promisor should reasonably expect to induce action or forbearance on the part of the promisee or a third person and which does induce such action or forbearance is binding if injustice can be avoided only by enforcement of the promise. O.C.G.A. § 13-3-44 (a). The remedy granted for breach may be limited as justice requires." *Id.* For a promise to be one for which the promisor should reasonably expect the promisee to rely, the promise must be for a definite period. *See e.g., Barker v. CTC Sales Corp.*, 406 S.E.2d 88, cert. denied (Ga. 1991) (holding that promissory estoppel has no application where the promise relied on was for employment for an indefinite period).

Rule Synthesis

Rules do not always appear as neatly packaged declarative statements. Sometimes you will be presented with a statute or case(s) that clearly states the applicable Rule, and other times you will have to engage in Rule synthesis. Rule synthesis requires you to look at the body of applicable case law and extract common principles and reconcile discrepancies to pull together the Rule under which courts are operating; in other words, you need to succinctly describe how the courts apply the law. This requires a careful read of cases in which the writer must have an understanding and then distill the common legal and factual bases on which the courts made their decisions. You will write the Rule as a definitional statement in which, as appropriate, you will include elements (required parts of the Rule) or the factors the court considers and the weight to which it affords them.

Below is a simplified example of Rule synthesis using three sources to define the Rule for promissory estoppel.

Source 1

A case (or cases) that identifies promissory estoppel as requiring: a promise, detrimental reliance, and a result that the action induced by the reliance is such that injustice can be avoided only by enforcement of the promise.

Source 2

A case (or cases) that identifies that there does not have to be a per se promise; so long as the defendant makes a clear, unequivocal statement, it will suffice.

Source 3

A case (or cases) that states detrimental reliance requires not just that the promisee rely on the promise to his detriment, but that the reliance be reasonable in nature.

A resulting synthesized Rule: Promissory estoppel requires that there be a promise or clear, unequivocal statement that induces reasonable reliance that results in detriment to the promisee to the extent that injustice can be avoided only by enforcement of the promise.

A synthesized Rule sometimes overlaps with rule Explanation because the context—including the purpose and policies underlying the Rule—can both define and explain the Rule itself. For example, the below Rule statement for promissory estoppel defines the Rule in part by including its purpose.

Common Law Example (Synthesized Rule)

To satisfy the third element of a claim for promissory estoppel, a plaintiff must show that he reasonably relied on a representation made by the defendant, which induced him to abandon an existing right or influenced him to act or refrain from acting. *Friedman*, 126 A.2d at 653. The promissory estoppel approach applies to future promises and is a flexible doctrine. *Id.*; *Malaker*, 395 A.2d at 230. Because promissory estoppel rests on principles of fairness, courts typically treat the requirement of reasonable reliance as a question of fact reserved for the fact finder. *Friedman*, 126 A.2d at 646; RESTATEMENT OF CONTRACTS § 90.

When determining whether reliance on a promise is reasonable in a promissory estoppel claim, New Jersey courts look to several factors, including: the immediate circumstances surrounding the promise, the language of the promise, and external factors that could affect the reliability of the promise. *See Thomas v. Princeton Univ.*, No. A-0680-14T1, 2016 N.J. Super. Unpub. LEXIS 2515, at *1 (Super. Ct. App. Div. Nov. 23, 2016) (holding that a temporary employee's reliance on a promise of permanent employment was unreasonable, especially considering the promise was made two years prior); *see also Goldfarb v. Solimine*, No. A-3740-16T2, 2019 N.J. Super. LEXIS 1472, at *1, *28 (Super. Ct. App. Div. June 26, 2019) (holding that the plaintiff was reasonable in relying on a promise of employment because the job was to start immediately); *E. Orange Bd. of Educ. v. N.J. Sch. Const. Corp.*, 963 A.2d 865 (N.J. Super. Ct. App. Div. 2009) (holding that negative, external economic impacts can make it unreasonable to rely on a promise).

Note: If you are writing a multi-issue memorandum—it may be that there are numerous issues based on legal rules with multiple elements or factors that warrant their own CREACC—you will likely need to synthesize Rules for each legal issue.

END OF CHAPTER SUMMARY

- After outlining the legal issues, the writer should identify the governing Rule or Rules.
- Rules can be derived from a statute, case law, synthesis of statutory and case law, or synthesis of case law.
- In a multi-issue memorandum, the Rules may be derived from multiple factors or a law with multiple elements.

EIGHT

Rule Explanation

The element of CREACC that distinguishes exam writing from writing a legal document more than any other is the rule Explanation. A rule Explanation does exactly what the name suggests—it explains the Rule. The traditional IRAC structure for exams does not typically incorporate rule Explanation. However, in doctrinal courses, the functional equivalent of the rule Explanation stems from the cases you read throughout the semester that help you understand how the court applies the rules. By the time you get to your final exam, your professor will typically expect you to include a rule and then directly apply that rule to the exam hypothetical. When you write a legal document, you need to explain to your reader how courts have treated the rule of law, the facts on which the case turned, and the rationale underlying the holdings. The reader needs to understand how the court prioritizes information when rendering a decision, so that the reader will understand what the plaintiff needs to establish a prima facie claim.

> **PROF'S TIPS**
>
> The Rule and rule Explanation sometimes overlap. You cannot always make a clean break or distinction between the two.

Think of the rule Explanation as the section in which you will teach the law to a reader unfamiliar with how the Rule "works." This can include the purpose and policies underlying the Rule, and any other information that assists the reader in better understanding it. In a memoran-

PROF'S TIPS

Infra (a term used to cite future information) and supra (a term used to cite previous information) are terms that are frequently used in law review articles and some legal documents. These are not terms typically used in 1L legal writing classes, so avoid using them in your 1L documents.

dum, to the extent the writer uses secondary authority, that authority tends to be most helpful in providing the broader context for the reader before the writer inserts case illustrations (discussed *infra*). Context, including policy, is important. It helps the reader understand the rationale underlying the law and can play an important role in shaping the writer's legal positions.

However, I caution against an over-reliance on policy. Indeed, I do not discuss policy much in the first semester of my legal writing course. Why not? Students tend to gravitate toward policy—and the discussion of policy often morphs into opinion. While I would never issue a blanket ban on incorporating policy into the first semester of legal writing, I sometimes joke, "If you give 1Ls policy rope, they think themselves policy cowboys." Always remember, you are in law school and not opinion or policy school. The focus of your writing in a memorandum should be to illustrate how the courts apply the law, followed by a prediction with respect to how a court would treat the issue you are analyzing. This book revisits the policy discussion in Part II: Persuasive Writing, where it will address how to effectively incorporate policy into legal argument.

One of the most effective ways to predict how a court will treat an issue is by understanding how the court has handled similar issues in the past. The primary way to do this is through what are commonly referred to as "case illustrations." A case illustration is similar to the case briefs you write for your doctrinal classes in that it includes the holding on a particular issue, the facts on which the court's decision was based, and the rationale underlying the court's decision.

Case Selection

One of the most common questions my writing students ask is "How many cases are enough?" Alas, consistent with my law faculty colleagues, my go-to professor answer is, "It depends." More specifically, my answer is, "Provide enough cases and illustrations so that the reader can truly understand what the law is and how the courts apply it." I know that my students may be inwardly rolling their eyes, but they are polite enough to keep that to themselves. I am not trying to "hide the ball." There truly is no "bright line rule" with respect to case selection and number; that answer depends on how much explanation and case illustration is necessary to clarify the Rule and the complexity of the law for the reader. More complicated issues may require more explanation, and accordingly necessitate more case illustrations.

When researching cases on a legal issue, look for cases with strong rule statements and cases that help you—and ultimately your reader—understand the rule underlying the legal issue. That may, where appropriate, include cases that provide the purpose and policy underlying the Rule. Certainly, for case illustrations you should seek cases with fact patterns that are comparable to the fact pattern at issue. This is true for both your authority (cases that support your legal position) and counter-authority (cases with holdings contrary to the position you selected).

Your job is to present the cases so that they paint a clear picture of the law for your reader. That means more than merely summarizing a series of cases; the writer needs to synthesize the information so that reader understands how the cases connect to the law and to each other. That means extracting information from cases that highlight the factual and legal bases of the judicial decisions. Include context beyond premises; include transitions that demonstrate how the cases under a premise relate to each other. If multiple cases have the same holding and rationale, it likely makes sense to discuss those cases together.

In summarizing the factual basis on which the court based its decision, the names of the parties are meaningless to the reader; use generic descriptions that have legal significance as it relates to the legal issue. For example, the descriptive word "plaintiff" will have greater significance than the proper name "Ms. Jones" if you are discussing a slip-and-fall situation. Similarly, terms like "store owner" and "patron" are more helpful to the reader's understanding of the case than proper names like "Mr. Hicks" and "Mr. James."

A Note about Persuasive Authority

In a document that aims to predict a legal outcome, the basis of that prediction should be as solid as possible. Mandatory authority provides a more solid foundation on which to make predictions, but persuasive authority can assist the reader in understanding the Rule where the mandatory authority is lacking. You may notice that the examples in this book incorporate unpublished cases. The caveat is that the reader should clearly understand that the authority is not binding. The Rule you adopt should come from mandatory authority if it exists, but you can use persuasive authority to illustrate how the courts implement that Rule.

For example, in the text of the sentence a writer can certainly note that the court adopted, relied on, or quoted another jurisdiction. What you should not do is rely on a case from another jurisdiction without pointing out in the text of the discussion that the authority is not binding. Otherwise, use of the case could mislead the reader. Your effectiveness as a legal writer is largely based on your ability to support your legal position. Writing about a case as though it is binding when it is not will damage the credibility of your position; merely citing the persuasive authority is not enough to point the distinction out to the reader.

Persuasive authority can be particularly helpful in explaining complex aspects of the law that mandatory authority may not clearly set forth. If you are specifically looking at non-mandatory case authority, that authority can also serve to fill in gaps of understanding where you are writing about an issue of first impression, or in jurisdictions where the common law is not well developed in the area of law you are researching.

Organizing the Rule and Rule Explanation to Prepare for Analysis

Charting the Case Law

For each legal issue, you may find it helpful to create a chart to organize your Rule and rule Explanation. The first column is the rule you have synthesized. If there is a macro-rule or one that includes elements or factors to consider, you should discuss each aspect separately (see Table 1). The second column includes how the court treated, or applied, the rule. You should include both the holdings that favor and do not favor the position you seek to support (authority and counter-authority). The information in the second column will serve as the basis of your rule Explanation. Finally, the third column will include facts from your case that are related to the rule you are discussing.

Include questions that you have and what you may need to incorporate into your application of that rule. Comparing and distinguishing columns two and three serves as the basis of your Analysis and Counter-

Analysis. This exercise is a note-taking organizational technique, so do not worry about it being "pretty." Focus on including information necessary to further your understanding of the rule and its application.

Table 1 focuses on reasonable reliance and its connection to the conditions underlying a promise. To assist you in making distinctions, I left the rule without emphasis, italicized the information that will be used in the rule Explanation, and bolded the information that will later be in your Analysis.

TABLE 1.

Rule	Case Treatment	Facts From Your Case
Reasonable reliance as part of promissory estoppel requires an examination of context, including factors such as: conditions, immediate circumstances, language of promise, external factors		
When the plaintiff meets conditions, there may be reasonable reliance	*In* Royal, *the plaintiff-tenants meet the reasonable reliance requirement when despite a no pet policy, a landlord allowed them to keep a dog on the condition they controlled it. Since the plaintiffs controlled the dog, the court held it was reasonable for them to rely on the defendant-landlord's promise.*	**The condition in this situation was that Li had to have a high G.P.A. If he meets that condition, then it may have been reasonable to rely on the promise.**
	In Malaker, *the court held that the language of the condition was too broad for a reasonable person to rely on it.*	**Was the condition specific enough? Is there a common understanding of "high G.P.A."?**
	In Bonczek, *the plaintiff was promised a position based on a positive reference check. Because the plaintiff embellished his background, he did not meet the conditions of the employer; therefore, there was no reasonable reliance.*	**On the one hand, there may be an argument that the drop in Li's G.P.A. means that it was not reasonable to rely on the promise. On the other hand, he was still on the Dean's List so that may be a standard for a high G.P.A.**

Organize by Premise, Not by Case

With few exceptions, each paragraph of your rule Explanation should begin with a thesis sentence. I call these sentences *premises*. A premise is not just a descriptive topic sentence. Instead, it is a sentence that summarizes how the court treats the Rule; those premise sentences are followed by case illustrations that support the premise (see *infra* for more discussion of case illustrations in a rule Explanation). Whenever you are discussing a distinct aspect of the law, a new topic warrants a new paragraph. Although one topic can span multiple paragraphs, do not try to include multiple topics in one paragraph unless it is a roadmap that serves to introduce the multiple topics that will ensue.

> **PROF'S TIPS**
> When reviewing your writing, if you see any paragraph longer than two-thirds to three-quarters of a page, see whether you can break it up.

Using the Chart to Organize by Premise

While a chart is a tool and not a requirement for organizing case law, it can provide a helpful visual when extracting the fact-based holding and rationale from the cases. Once you chart the cases for your issue, try to extract from the fact-based holdings and rationales or principles that you can develop into premise sentences. For example, using the cases from Table 1, you could create three premises under which you can include a number of cases. From the *Royal* case, you may create a premise that "[w]hen the promisor creates a condition that the promisee meets, a court is more likely to find the promisee's reliance to be reasonable."

After creating this premise sentence, cite *Royal* and any other cases (via a string citation) that support the premise; you can then include not only a case illustration of *Royal*, but also case illustrations from other cases that support the premise. With respect to *Malaker*, the second case in Table 1, the premise could be a transition sentence for counter-authority or begin a new paragraph. "To the contrary, when a promisee fails to meet the condition set forth by the promisor, he no longer has reason to rely on the promisor." Then cite *Malaker* and any other cases that support that premise; follow the premise with case illustrations. *Bonaker* is a case that could be part of that string citation after the premise you created for *Malaker*; you can also use *Malaker* as a second case illustration for that premise.

> **PROF'S TIPS**
> You can use the same case to illustrate various premises. Do not be afraid to use a case more than once.

As I evaluate student papers, I look to see whether there is a logical flow in the substance and style of the writing. Nothing screams emerging legal writer than seeing the name of a case in the text of a sentence that begins the paragraph. One way to check the macro-organization of your rule Explanation is by reading the first sentence in every one of its paragraphs to see whether it tells a coherent story about how the law works with respect to the legal issue in question.

The following are the premises from the sample memorandum's rule Explanation of reasonable reliance:

- The court looks to the context—including the specific language and conditions—of the promise to determine whether it was reasonable to rely on the promise.
- Conversely, where the conditions of the promise are clear, but the plaintiff fails to meet them, the court will not find reasonable reliance.
- When the factors leading to the promisor breaking the promise are within the promisor's control, it may be reasonable to rely on the promise.
- When the promise is made in an indefinite situation, such as when the expected performance is remote in time or when the promise is made under uncertain economic circumstances, it is not reasonable to rely on the promise.
- When economic circumstances affect the viability of a promise, it is not reasonable to rely on promises.

Below is an excerpt from the sample memorandum at the end of this section. Notice that there is a synthesized rule that the writer has assembled from all the cases she used. She also created premise sentences and used the facts, holdings, and rationales from case law to support them. Consistent with Table 1 in this chapter, I left the rule without emphasis and italicized the rule Explanation. Remember, case illustrations are examples that detail how the court applies the rule. They "illustrate" the premise.

> When determining whether reliance on a promise is reasonable in a promissory estoppel claim, New Jersey courts look to several factors, including: the immediate circumstances surrounding the promise, the language of the promise, and external factors that could affect the reliability of the promise.

The court looks to the context—including the specific language and conditions—of the promise to determine whether it was reasonable to rely on the promise. When the promisee meets the conditions to receive the benefit of a promise and the promisor takes actions that would lead a reasonable person to believe he would receive the benefit, the court may uphold reasonable reliance in a promissory estoppel claim. For example, in Royal, *a landlord had a no pets policy for his tenants, but he gave "special permission" to the plaintiffs to keep their dog so long as they controlled it. After several years of allowing the pet to remain on the premises, the landlord attempted to force the plaintiffs to give up their dog. The landlord admitted he had never seen the dog off a leash and that the plaintiffs complied with all conditions. The tenants could likely have made alternative arrangements to live elsewhere or decide not to buy a pet, but did so in reliance on the defendant's clear and definite promise that the tenant's dog would be allowed without trouble.* Id. *Because the plaintiffs met all the conditions of the promise and were allowed to bond with the dog for years, the court held that it was reasonable they relied on the landlord's promise that they could keep their dog.* Id.

PROF'S TIPS

Note that "court" is not capitalized. "Court" is capitalized when it is part of a proper noun, when you are referring to the Supreme Court, or when you are submitting the document to the court in question, as in "This Court should affirm the ..." (see the brief).

Conversely, where the conditions of the promise are clear, but the plaintiff fails to meet them, the court will not find reasonable reliance. In Bonczek, *the plaintiff was offered employment contingent upon the completion of reference checks establishing a generally positive character. The plaintiff embellished his title and salary with his previous employer, which raised concerns about his credibility. The court held that because the promise was contingent on specific conditions that the plaintiff did not meet, there was no valid promissory estoppel claim.*

Citation as an Important Organizing Tool

Citation can be a helpful organizing principle, especially in the rule Explanation. I know I promised that I would not teach you citation, and I am (mostly) keeping that promise. However, there are things about citation I highlight to help you organize your writing and can even provide a checklist. One of these organizing principles is that when you cite a case for the *first* time, you must cite it in its entirety; you cannot split it (separate the case name from the rest of the citation) or include a short-form citation. If there is a full citation in the text of a sentence, it signals that the writer organized by case rather than by issue. Unless the document is about a case, it should be organized by topic.

PROF'S TIPS
Check to see whether your professor requires you to either underline or italicize in your citations.

PROF'S TIPS
When you are first drafting your memo, use the full citation every time (you can cut and paste while inserting the appropriate page number each time). You will not be confused as to the source as you organize and re-organize your memo.

Everyone Loves Good Explanatory Parentheticals

After each premise, there should be a single case or string citation of the cases that support that premise. If you have not already cited the case in the roadmap or in a Rule statement, this is where you typically include the full citations; it is also a good place to include explanatory parentheticals. Explanatory parentheticals are for information that is not necessary to the text of the sentence, so do not include in an explanatory parenthetical information that is necessary to explain the Rule or information that you will later incorporate into your Analysis. Their purpose is to concisely convey case relevance to the reader, and when used correctly, they are both efficient and efficacious. A parenthetical is particularly helpful when you are citing a case only for a Rule statement or when you are citing a case that supports a proposition, but you are not planning to use the case for a case illustration.

PROF'S TIPS
Information that you are going to include in the Analysis section of your discussion should not be hidden in explanatory parentheticals; remember, the information is included in the parenthetical as extraneous.

Explanatory parentheticals usually begin with a word in the present progressive tense or a gerund. Common first words in an explanatory parenthetical include "holding," "arguing," "describing," and "explaining." However, in a memorandum, you will most often use the word "holding" and include the factual basis. Below is an example.

PROF'S TIPS

Explanatory parentheticals almost always follow citation signals unless the writer uses details of the case in the text to illustrate the premise.

The court looks to the context—including the specific language and conditions—of the promise to determine whether it was reasonable to rely on the promise. *Malaker*, 395 A.2d at 230 (holding that there was no valid claim for promissory estoppel because a reasonable person would not rely on a promise with very few specifics discussed).

In the case illustrations that follow your explanatory parentheticals, you will likely detail the cases that you cited in your premises, roadmap, or Rule; you can now cite those cases in short form. Below are two examples that illustrate the effectiveness of organizing by premise. In the first example the writer began the paragraph with a premise. She then string cited two cases that supported that premise; the first case was cited for the first time and was appropriately cited in its entirety, and the second case is a short-form citation (because it was not cited for the first time) followed by an explanatory parenthetical. The second example does not begin with a premise. Instead, the writer describes a case without context. Because the writer is citing the case for the first time, she correctly cited it in its entirety. As you can see, not only is the case lacking context, its long citation in the text of the sentence is disruptive to the text of the sentence.

Write This (Premise before Case Illustration)

PROF'S TIPS

Using the words "For example" or their equivalent is a reminder that you are using the case illustrations as examples of the legal concept you introduced. Of course, you do not have to use "for example" every time you use a case illustration.

When the factors leading to the promisor breaking the promise are within the promisor's control, it may be reasonable to rely on the promise. *Pop's Cones, Inc. v. Resorts Intern. Hotel, Inc.*, 704 A.2d 1321, 1326 (N.J. Super. Ct. App. Div. 1998); *see also Peck*, 679 A.2d at 745 (holding that an employee reasonably relied on an oral offer for a full-time position that was subsequently rescinded because the decision was based only on the employer's change of mind about the employee's fit). For example, in *Pop's Cones*, a casino induced a store owner to give up her lease at her current location to relocate to the casino. 704 A.2d at 1326. The store owner repeatedly told the casino the time by which she needed to renew her current lease. *Id.* at 1322. The casino told the store owner not to renew her lease and to "pack up … and plan on moving." *Id.* Because virtually nothing remained to be determined by the parties, the casino told the store owner to "pack up," and it was at the casino's sole discretion to back out of the promise, the court held that there was a valid claim of promissory estoppel and it was reasonable for the store owner to rely on the promise. *Id.* at 1326.

Not That (Case Illustration without Context)

In *Pop's Cones, Inc. v. Resorts Intern Hotel Inc.*, 704 A.2d 1321, 1326 (N.J. Super. Ct. App. Div. 1998), a casino induced

PROF'S TIPS

A case name in the first sentence of a paragraph is a red flag. In a rule Explanation, you are using cases to illustrate concepts. Without the context of these concepts you are merely presenting a series of case briefs. That is not nearly as useful to your reader who is trying to understand that context.

In addition, the full citation, though correct, is an eyesore and makes your sentence more difficult to read. Citing your premise allows you to put your citation in a citation sentence and use short-form citation in the text of your sentence.

a store owner to give up her lease at her current location to relocate to the casino. The store owner repeatedly told the casino the time by which she needed to renew her current lease. *Id.* at 1322. The casino told the store owner not to renew her lease and to "pack up … and plan on moving." *Id.* Because virtually nothing remained to be determined by the parties, the casino told the store owner to "pack up," and it was at the casino's sole discretion to back out of the promise, the court held that there was a valid claim of promissory estoppel, and it was reasonable for the store owner to rely on the promise. *Id.* at 1326.

Authority versus Counter-Authority

Once the rule Explanation sets for the reader the continuum on which a court regards a legal concept, the reader will better understand in Analysis where the facts of the current situation fall on that continuum. Accordingly, after providing a Rule or definition for the concept, the case illustrations should begin with illustrations that support your legal position (authority) and then illustrate with cases that do not support your legal position (counter-authority).

Begin discussing a legal concept by not only defining it, but by also illustrating where a court found support for that concept. After illustrating cases with holdings in which the court upheld the legal claim related to that issue, include case illustrations that demonstrate where the court held that there was insufficient support for that claim. Do not only include cases with holdings that support your predicted outcome; you must also include cases with holdings that support the opposite legal conclusion, because ultimately you will engage in both analysis that supports your legal prediction and counter-analysis for the legal position that does not.

> **PROF'S TIPS**
>
> If you find yourself including more authority that supports an outcome that is contrary to your prediction, you should either reevaluate whether your legal prediction is viable or provide additional case support for your position.

For example, if you are writing a memorandum with a CREACC on detrimental reliance, you should begin by defining detrimental reliance; that is your Rule statement. How you proceed immediately after defining the term depends on whether your research has led you to conclude that there is or is not detrimental reliance. If your writing will support that there is detrimental reliance, you will follow that definition with illustrations where the court concluded that there was support for detrimental reliance followed by illustrations in which the court came to the opposite holding.

The following is an example of how to structure the rule Explanation in which the author has concluded that there is a substantial detriment. Notice that after defining the term "substantial detriment," the author begins with illustrations of what is substantial detriment (the authority to support the author's position) followed by examples of what the courts have held not to be substantial detriment (counter-authority).

Where a promisee is prevented from obtaining all or most of the benefit of a promise, the court is likely to find a substantial detriment. *Onorato Const., Inc. v. Eastman Const. Co.*, 711 A.2d 1363 (N.J. Super. Ct. App. Div. 1998); *see also King James Care Ctr. of Chatham 415 S. Blvd. Chatham v. Richardson*, 2018 N.J. Super. Unpub. LEXIS 4394 at *25–26 (holding that where the daughter of a nursing home resident neglected to pay any of the outstanding balance, there was a substantial detriment). For example, in *Onorato*, the plaintiff and subcontractor told the general contractor that the subcontractor was in financial difficulties and the general contractor should either pay the plaintiff directly or issue a joint check. 711 A.2d at 1364. The general contractor acknowledged he would do so, sent a portion of the payment as a joint check, but then later sent the rest to the subcontractor alone, who was insolvent. *Id.* Because the general contractor knew of the issues, acknowledged them orally and in writing, yet issued only one check as a joint payment, the court held that there was a substantial detriment. *Id.* at 1365–66. Likewise, when the promisee has no other option but to rely on the promisor's assertions, the court may find a substantial detriment. *King James*, 2018 N.J. Super. Unpub. LEXIS 4394 at **25–26. In *King James*, the daughter of a patient in a nursing home explicitly asserted that she was not personally liable for her mother's payments to the nursing home. *Id.* at *3. However, she had power of attorney over her mother and previously assured the nursing home that she would "promptly" fill out the necessary Medicaid paperwork and would pay for the remaining balance of her mother's care from her mother's assets. *Id.* at *3, *5. The court held that because the daughter allowed two years of payments to accrue while assuring the nursing home she would be responsible for the payments if Medicaid did not pay them, the nursing home incurred a substantial detriment for which the daughter was responsible. *Id.* at **25–26.

> **PROF'S TIPS**
> This is a premise for substantial detriment.

> **PROF'S TIPS**
> This case illustrates the premise.

> **PROF'S TIPS**
> This transition presents another aspect of the premise on substantial detriment; a case illustration follows it.

> **PROF'S TIPS**
> This premise sets up the counter-authority. The writer is including cases where the court did not find support for substantial detriment. A case illustration follows.

The non-exercise of a right to seek opportunity elsewhere is not a substantial detriment that supports a claim of detrimental reliance. *Malaker*, 395 A.2d at 232; *see also Friedman*, 126 A.2d at 652 (holding that where the plaintiff held land to be sold at a special price to a buyer, but the buyer later backed out, there was no detriment because the seller expended nothing and could still sell to someone else). For instance, in *Malaker*, a corporation's stockholder committee sued a bank alleging the bank made an oral promise to loan the corporation money, which it failed to do. 395 A.2d at 224. The corporation alleged it could have received funds elsewhere had it not relied on the bank's promise. *Id.* at 232. However, the court held there was no proof the corporation could have been successful in seeking loans elsewhere. *Id.* Ultimately, the court held the forbearance from seeking funding from other sources in reliance on the bank's promise to supply a loan was not sufficiently substantial to show detriment. *Id.*

> **PROF'S TIPS**
> Again, this is another premise to set up the case illustration for what constitutes no substantial detriment.

Moreover, where the promisee receives most of the benefits of a promise, there is likely no substantial detriment. *Sadej*, 2019 N.J. Super. Unpub. LEXIS 1043 at *22. For instance, the plaintiffs in *Sadej* received zoning permits to make improvements to their home. *Id.* at *2. When they completed about 80% of the work, the city issued a stop order, saying the improvements did not comply with the permits. *Id.* The couple still completed most of the improvements (except for attaching their detached garage), was only held up for seven days, and received income from renting out the property. *Id.* at *23–24. Because the delay was minimal and the majority of projects were still completed, the court determined there was no substantial detriment. *Id.*

The following is an example of how to structure the rule Explanation in which the author has concluded that there is no detriment. Notice that after defining the term "substantial detriment," the author begins with illustrations of what is *not* substantial detriment (the authority to support the author's position) followed by examples of what the courts have held to be substantial detriment (counter-authority).

Where a promisee is prevented from obtaining all or most of the benefit of a promise, the court is likely to find a substantial detriment. *Onorato Const., Inc. v. Eastman Const. Co.*, 711 A.2d 1363 (N.J. Super. Ct. App. Div. 1998); *see also King James Care Ctr. of Chatham 415 S. Blvd. Chatham v. Richardson*, 2018 N.J. Super. Unpub. LEXIS 4394 at *25–26 (holding that where the daughter of a nursing home resident neglected to pay any of the outstanding balance, there was a substantial detriment). However, the non-exercise of a right to seek opportunity elsewhere is not a substantial detriment that supports a claim of detrimental reliance. *Malaker*, 395 A.2d at 232; *see also Friedman*, 126 A.2d at 652 (holding that where the plaintiff held land to be sold at a special price to a buyer, but the buyer later backed out, there was no detriment because the seller expended nothing and could still sell to someone else). For instance, in *Malaker*, a corporation's stockholder committee sued a bank alleging the bank made an oral promise to loan the corporation money, which it failed to do. 395 A.2d at 224. The corporation alleged it could have received funds elsewhere had it not relied on the bank's promise. *Id.* at 232. However, the court held there was no proof the corporation could have been successful in seeking loans elsewhere. *Id.* Ultimately, the court held the forbearance from seeking funding from other sources in reliance on the bank's promise to supply a loan was not sufficiently substantial to show detriment. *Id.*

> **PROF'S TIPS**
> This is a premise for substantial detriment.

> **PROF'S TIPS**
> This premise sets up the topic by defining it, but the writer transitions to cases that illustrate where the court did not find support for substantial detriment.

Moreover, where the promisee receives most of the benefits of a promise, there is likely no substantial detriment. *Sadej*, 2019 N.J. Super. Unpub. LEXIS 1043 at *22. For instance, the plaintiffs in *Sadej* received zoning permits to make improvements to their home. *Id.* at *2. When they completed about 80% of the work, the city issued a

> **PROF'S TIPS**
> Again, this is another premise to set up the case illustration for where there is no substantial detriment.

stop order, saying the improvements did not comply with the permits. *Id.* The couple still completed most of the improvements (except for attaching their detached garage), was only held up for seven days, and received income from renting out the property. *Id.* at *23–24. Because the delay was minimal and the majority of projects were still completed, the court determined there was no substantial detriment. *Id.*

To the contrary, when the promisee does not receive the benefit of a promise, there may be a substantial detriment that supports a claim of promissory estoppel. *Onorato*, 711 A.2d 1363. For example, in *Onorato* the plaintiff and subcontractor told the general contractor that the subcontractor was in financial difficulties and the general contractor should either pay the plaintiff directly or issue a joint check. *Id.* at 1364. The general contractor acknowledged he would do so, sent a portion of the payment as a joint check, but then later sent the rest to the subcontractor alone, who was insolvent. *Id.* Because the general contractor knew of the issues, acknowledged them orally and in writing, yet issued only one check as a joint payment, the court held that there was a substantial detriment. *Id.* at 1365–66. Likewise, when the promisee has no other option but to rely on the promisor's assertions, the court may find a substantial detriment. *King James*, 2018 N.J. Super. LEXIS 4394 at *25–26. In *King James*, the daughter of a patient in a nursing home explicitly asserted that she was not personally liable for her mother's payments to the nursing home. *Id.* at *3. However, she had power of attorney over her mother and previously assured the nursing home that she would "promptly" fill out the necessary Medicaid paperwork and would pay for the remaining balance of her mother's care from her mother's assets. *Id.* at *3, *5. The court held that because the daughter allowed two years of payments to accrue while assuring the nursing home she would be responsible for the payments if

PROF'S TIPS

This case illustrates the premise for the counter-authority.

PROF'S TIPS

This transition presents another aspect of the premise on substantial detriment; a case illustration follows it.

Medicaid did not pay them, the nursing home incurred a substantial detriment for which the daughter was responsible. *Id.* at *25–26.

Do Not Overuse Quotes

In their initial foray into legal writing, it is not uncommon for students to rely heavily on quotation. I suppose the thinking is that the court expressed its opinion better than the student ever could. Even assuming that is true, the reader expects the writer to present the meaning and impact of the courts' opinions; that requires synthesis. Part of the effectiveness of the rule Explanation is your ability to explain the law to your reader. That requires that you synthesize the information. No one wants to read a series of quotations. As a general rule, use quotes only when the language appears frequently (as in a term of art), or is so well stated that you cannot effectively paraphrase it.

END OF CHAPTER SUMMARY

- As its name suggests, the rule Explanation explains the Rule.
- Sometimes the line between Rule and rule Explanation is blurry. This is particularly true as common law interpretation can be incorporated into the Rule itself.
- The rule Explanation is organized by premises, a form of topic sentences.
- Use case illustrations (facts, holding, and rationale) to demonstrate how courts have interpreted the Rule in your CREACC.
- In your rule Explanation, after you set out a definition or Rule, you should organize the section by beginning with the case illustrations with holdings that support your position, followed by counter-authority, or authority in which the court came to the opposite conclusion on your issue. Again, in case illustrations it is important to include not only the holdings, but also the factual basis for the holdings and the courts' rationale. That information is critical to your Analysis section.

NINE

Analysis

Rule Analysis—sometimes called rule Application—is the heart of legal writing. In the context of the memorandum, rule Analysis follows rule Explanation in which the writer has presumptively taught the reader how courts understand and treat the rule of law at issue. After the rule Explanation details the law surrounding an issue and places it on a legal continuum, the rule Analysis predicts the strength of a legal claim by comparing and distinguishing the facts of the current legal situation with the fact-based holding of precedent.

You will organize the Analysis by assertion—in other words, by your legal conclusion with respect to each premise. Although there does not have to be a 1:1 correlation, there should be symmetry between the rule Explanation and Analysis section because the Analysis should generally follow the topical organization of the rule Explanation. The premises and corresponding assertions from the promissory estoppel memorandum are in Table 1. In the set of premises and assertions, the first premise summarizes the general Rule, and every premise thereafter discusses a specific aspect of that Rule. For each premise (aspect of the Rule the writer addresses) there is often a corresponding assertion. Remember, just as in your rule Explanation, in the Analysis section, the first sentence of each paragraph should not typically include a case name; it will instead be an assertion.

Table 1 includes excerpts of the memorandum at the end of this section. Notice the parallel between the premises in the rule Explanation and the assertions in the Analysis.

PROF'S TIPS

Look for symmetry in the organization of the rule Explanation to the Analysis.

TABLE 1.

Premises for Reasonable Reliance	Assertions for Reasonable Reliance
The court looks to the context—including the specific language and conditions—of the promise to determine whether it was reasonable to rely on the promise.	[There is no assertion for this premise because the premise summarizes a rule for reasonable reliance.]
Conversely, where the conditions of the promise are clear, but the plaintiff fails to meet them, the court will not find reasonable reliance.	Mr. Li likely cannot support a claim of promissory estoppel because it was not reasonable for Mr. Li to rely on Micheo & Yoon's promise of future employment if he did not meet the law firm's conditions to Mr. Li's post-graduation employment.
When the factors leading to the promisor breaking the promise are within the promisor's control, it may be reasonable to rely on the promise.	Mr. Li could claim he met the conditions of the agreement. He was still on the Dean's List, he was on journal, and he worked for Micheo & Yoon during his second summer.
When the promise is made in an indefinite situation, such as when the expected performance is remote in time or when the promise is made under uncertain economic circumstances, it is not reasonable to rely on the promise.	It was not reasonable for Mr. Li to rely on Micheo & Yoon's promise of employment because the promise was made too distant in time from its expected fulfillment.
When economic circumstances affect the viability of a promise, it is not reasonable to rely on promises.	The external economic forces that affected the law firm's ability to deliver on its promise were likely such that it was unreasonable for Mr. Li to rely on the promise of employment.

Notably, contrary to the rule Explanation in which the premise is followed sometimes immediately by case illustrations, the assertions are followed by the facts of the legal situation. The writer should then integrate case comparisons to cases with holdings that support the position you adopted (see examples below).

> **PROF'S TIPS**
> Do not include in your Analysis cases that you have not first discussed in your rule Explanation. You can discuss cases in your rule Explanation that you do not incorporate in your Analysis, but not the reverse.

Write This (An Assertion Followed by Supporting Facts that Eventually Integrate the Law)

Mr. Li likely cannot support a claim of promissory estoppel because it was not reasonable for Mr. Li to rely on Micheo & Yoon's promise of future employment if he did not meet the law firm's conditions to Mr. Li's post-graduation employment. Ms. Heinan specifically told Mr. Li that he had to keep up a "high G.P.A." in order to receive an offer in his last year of law school. Mr. Li had a G.P.A. of 3.8 at the time Ms. Heinan made the promise, but he purposefully decided to "relax" his work ethic and allowed his G.P.A to drop to a 3.5. When the promisee does not satisfy the conditions of the promise, the court is unlikely to hold that reliance on the promise is reasonable. *Bonczek*, 701 A.2d at 744. Like in *Bonczek*, *id.*, where plaintiff failed to establish promissory estoppel when he failed to meet the employment's condition he receive positive references, Mr. Li's employment was conditioned, in part, on a high G.P.A.

> **PROF'S TIPS**
> When you proofread your memorandum, glance at the Analysis sections to see whether there are underlines or italics—whichever you choose for case citation. If you see large stretches without either, it may mean that you are not using cases to support your assertions. That would be a problem since much of Analysis is about comparing and contrasting the facts of your case to the fact-based holding and rationale to precedent.

> **PROF'S TIPS**
> Note that when you are comparing the facts of a case to facts from your situation, include the citation immediately after the case name rather than at the end of the sentence; that way the citation does not appear to also include the facts of your case.

Not This (The Assertion Followed Immediately by a Case Comparison to Facts the Writer Has Not Yet Set Forth)

> Mr. Li likely cannot support a claim of promissory estoppel because it was not reasonable for Mr. Li to rely on Micheo & Yoon's promise of future employment if he did not meet the law firm's conditions to Mr. Li's post-graduation employment. Like in *Bonczek*, *id.*, where plaintiff failed to establish promissory estoppel when he failed to meet the employment's condition he receive positive references, Mr. Li's employment was conditioned, in part, on a high G.P.A.

Because facts are critical to the outcome of the case, analogical reasoning is the crux of the Analysis. If the facts of the current legal situation are more like the facts of precedent where a court upheld a claim on an issue, then it is more likely that a court will also uphold the current claim on the same issue. Include the fact-based holding and rationale of each case you compare to the facts of your situation.

PROF'S TIPS

When reviewing both rule Explanation and Analysis, I look for the words "held" and "because" to ensure that, in the discussion of precedent, the writer included a fact-based holding and rationale.

Although you have included that information in the rule Explanation, your reader should never have to turn pages to understand what you are saying. Consider your description of case law in the Analysis section to be a "refresher." Only bring in the information necessary for the comparison, but those comparisons should be full or complete. If you make a factual comparison to a case, the reader should understand what the court held and why in that case, so that you can predict that a court is likely to draw the same conclusion for the same reason in this situation.

Repeat in your Analysis terms of art or key language to strengthen connections. For example, if in your rule Explanation courts repeatedly describe the shift in behavior for detrimental reliance as needing to be compelling, the word "compelling" should be a reference in the Analysis section.

Look at the following examples of comparisons within Analysis. Please note that where there is a case citation in the first sentence it is because the excerpt is from the middle of a paragraph and not at its start.

This (Factual Comparison in a Single Sentence)

Just as in *Malaker, id.* at 232, where the court held forgoing alternative funding prospects in reliance on the bank's promise was too speculative to be substantial, when Mr. Li failed to seek alternative employment, he precluded any opportunity to determine whether he would have received another job offer from a top law firm, and how much he would have made there.

PROF'S TIPS

Not all professors require full comparisons in the Analysis section. Pay attention to your professor's requirements.

Or This (Factual Comparison in Multiple Sentences)

Mr. Li had a G.P.A. of 3.8 at the time Ms. Heinan made the promise, but he purposefully decided to "relax" his work ethic and allowed his G.P.A to drop to a 3.5. When the promisee does not satisfy the conditions of the promise, the court is unlikely to hold that reliance on the promise is reasonable. *Bonczek*, 701 A.2d at 744. Like in *Bonczek, id.*, where plaintiff failed to establish promissory estoppel when he failed to meet the employment's condition that he receive positive references, Mr. Li's employment was conditioned, in part, on a high G.P.A. While Mr. Li's 3.5 G.P.A. is slightly above the 3.45 G.P.A. required to make the Dean's List, it is a G.P.A. that Micheo & Yoon and similarly ranked firms do not consider "high," thus Mr. Li has not met the condition of a "high G.P.A."

Not This (Classic Incomplete Comparison):

The offer from Micheo & Yoon influenced Mr. Li to work for the firm his second summer in reliance on their promise to employ him after he graduated from law school. Like the plaintiff in *Peck*, 679 A.2d at 753, Mr. Li made arrangements in reliance on his acceptance of said employment offer—he ensured that he fulfilled the requirements Micheo & Yoon had clearly stated as conditions to his working for their firm and did not explore other viable opportunities.

PROF'S TIPS

This is not a true comparison and is an example of one of my common frustrations when I read Analysis. How is the plaintiff in *Peck* like Mr. Li? Was the holding in *Peck* with respect to reliance favorable to the plaintiff? What was the rationale for that holding and how would it likely apply to Mr. Li?

END OF CHAPTER SUMMARY

- The Analysis will always appear in a new paragraph after the rule Explanation.
- Just as the rule Explanation is organized by premises, the Analysis is organized by assertions, which are conclusions based on the premises.
- The assertion is followed by factual support of the situation; those are the facts from your legal situation, not case law. Begin to insert case law to compare the fact-based holding and rationale of the case to the facts of the legal situation.
- Fully compare case law to the facts of the legal situation.

TEN

Counter-Analysis

Most legal writing professors do not use an acronym that includes a letter for Counter-Analysis; instead, it is an inherent part of Analysis. I include a C for Counter-Analysis because I like to highlight its importance. Why would you want to highlight Counter-Analysis in a memorandum? Unlike a persuasive document where the goal is to obfuscate information contrary to what the writer advocates, in a memorandum the writer is writing an objective prediction. Therefore, it is important that the writer point out both sides of the legal position and then demonstrate why one side was stronger than the other.

You cannot prepare a complete Analysis without including, addressing, and responding to any weaknesses of the position you identified as strongest. Remember, it is okay if the position you adopt as strongest is not that of your client. Your role as the memorandum's author is to assess the viability of a legal position, not to argue it. Every good offense needs to anticipate the defense and vice versa. This is where you identify the position that you think is weaker.

PROF'S TIPS

If you find yourself including more Counter-Analysis than Analysis, you should either reevaluate whether your legal prediction is viable or provide additional case support for your position.

Consistent with Analysis, the Counter-Analysis begins with an assertion; however, the format can vary. It can be helpful to highlight Counter-Analysis by pointing out arguments that are counter to the writer's legal prediction. That highlight would begin in a separate paragraph that would begin with language like "Mr. Li could assert" or "Mr. Li may argue." Alternatively, you can make effective Counter-Analysis in the same paragraph with the Analysis by making factual distinctions from counter-authority. Just as in your Analysis, following your assertion you should include facts first and then law to support the opposing position, and then integrate case comparisons that support it. Also consistent with the Analysis, include the fact-based holding and rationale from your counter-authority.

Once you have completed the Counter-Analysis, rebut it before concluding the CREACC, otherwise the reader will not understand which position is the stronger one. After rebutting the Counter-Analysis, then conclude your CREACC.

Below are two examples of Counter-Analysis. The first is one in which the author highlights the opposing argument by including it in a separate paragraph. Note that the writer includes the rebuttal in the same paragraph as the Counter-Analysis. The second example is a more subtle approach to Counter-Analysis in which the writer does not highlight the assertion as an opposing one, but instead distinguishes authority counter to her position. The latter approach is the one most commonly used in a persuasive document in which the writer does not wish to highlight the opposing position, but still must address authority that may weaken her position.

Example 1 (Counter-Analysis in a Separate Paragraph)

Mr. Li likely cannot establish that he suffered a definite detriment as a result of Micheo & Yoon's promise because his alleged damages are speculative as there is no way to calculate the exact damages Mr. Li incurred. In fact, the law firm could argue Mr. Li gained some benefit as a result of his experience with a top 100 law firm and the ability to stay in his home state during his summer associateships. For two years, Micheo & Yoon was diligent in giving Mr. Li a "big law" experience. The alleged detriment in this case is similar to that in *Village Square*, where the plaintiff could not establish that he could have achieved financial gain had he exercised alternative options because there was no way to establish what Village Square earned through alternatives to working with the plaintiff. 2016 N.J. Super. Unpub. LEXIS 269. Analogously, Mr. Li did not apply to any other law firm positions, so there is no way to prove he could have acquired a legal job of the same caliber and salary as Micheo & Yoon had he never relied on Ms. Heinan's promise and worked for the law firm over his second summer.

Mr. Li could try to establish a definite method to calculate his lost earnings by comparing the salary he would have made with Micheo & Yoon to his current salary. Mr. Li's salary with a solo practitioner is seventy-five percent less than the starting salary at Micheo & Yoon. When there is a clear way to prove economic loss, the court may find there is a definite detriment. *Goldfarb*, 2019 N.J. Super. LEXIS 1472 at *1, *29–30. In *Goldfarb*, the plaintiff used past earnings to establish a definite loss when he quit his job in reliance on the defendant's promise of employment. *Id.* However, unlike in *Goldfarb*, *id.* at *30, where the plaintiff could point to specific loss, Mr. Li had no past earnings and did not forgo current employment, so he did not give up a definite salary to work with Micheo & Yoon.

> **PROF'S TIPS**
> The Counter-Analysis offers an assertion for the other position followed by facts and then law to support it.

> **PROF'S TIPS**
> The writer then rebuts the Counter-Analysis by stating why the counter-position is not as strong as the position the writer identified as stronger.

Example 2 (Counter-Analysis in the Same Paragraph through Legal Distinction)

The external economic forces that affected the law firm's ability to deliver on its promise were likely such that it was unreasonable for Mr. Li to rely on the promise of employment.

At the time Ms. Heinan made the statement regarding possible future employment to Mr. Li, there was a moderate economic recession. When Ms. Heinan informed Mr. Li that the firm could no longer employ him, many firms were also experiencing a decrease in job availability due to the dip in the economy. In *E. Orange Bd. of Educ. v. N.J. Sch. Const. Corp.*, 963 A.2d 865, 874–75. (N.J. Super. Ct. App. Div. 2009), statewide funding cuts led to the SCC defunding certain school projects. In light of the dire funding issues for school projects across the state, it was not reasonable for the school's board to rely on promises that it would receive funding for their projects. *Id.* at 870. Similarly, Micheo & Yoon was likely affected by the negative effects that a recession can have on businesses nationwide. Ms. Heinan told Mr. Li the firm would be unable to hire him due to economic circumstances. In *Thomas*, the court held that when there are viable business reasons for not hiring someone and budgetary cutbacks, it is not reasonable to rely on a promise of employment. 2016 N.J. Super. Unpub. LEXIS 2515 at *9. The employer in *Thomas* had no new construction projects that would supply the funds necessary to hire new permanent employees. *Id.* at *4. Just as there needs to be funds to hire construction workers, a law firm would need the economic conditions to hire new lawyers. In the context of a slowing economy, which was evident at the time Ms. Heinan made the promise to Mr. Li, it would likely not be reasonable to rely on such a promise. Unlike the defendant in *Pop's Cones*, 704 A.2d at 1326, who was in complete control of the circumstances surrounding its promise, and in fact encouraged the plaintiff to continue to rely on its promises, an economic recession is not in the control of a law firm, and no one at the law firm explicitly continued to encourage Mr. Li to stay with the firm.

PROF'S TIPS

This example does not point out a counter-argument, but instead uses distinction for effective counter-analysis. This is especially effective in a persuasive document.

END OF CHAPTER SUMMARY

- Counter-Analysis begins in a paragraph separate from the Analysis. Like the Analysis, it begins with an assertion that is counter to the position you adopted. It can be what opposing counsel could assert, or if your client has the weaker position, what your client could assert.
- Just as in the Analysis, include facts from your situation and then use the counter-authority from the rule Explanation to support the counter-position.
- After setting up the counter-position, briefly rebut it by distinguishing the case law from your situation.

The Memorandum

MEMORANDUM

TO: Kamil Mkparu
FROM: Charli Davis & Mackenzie Ward
DATE: June 12, 2024
RE: Li v. Micheo & Yoon

QUESTION PRESENTED

1. Under New Jersey law, can Mr. Li support a claim of promissory estoppel against Micheo & Yoon, by establishing that his reliance on the law firm's promise of post-graduation employment made the summer after Mr. Li's first year was reasonable, and that this reliance resulted in definite and substantial detriment to Mr. Li?

> **PROF'S TIPS**
> This can be Question Presented or Issue Presented. If you are analyzing multiple questions, then you would make plural the word Question or Issue.

BRIEF ANSWER

1. No. In New Jersey, a prima facie claim for promissory estoppel requires, *inter alia*, the promisee to reasonably rely on the promise and then incur a definite and substantial detriment based on that reliance. While Mr. Li did rely on the firm's

> **PROF'S TIPS**
> If you are analyzing multiple issues, "Answer" should be plural.

promise, it was not reasonable to do so because the promise was for employment too far in the future, Mr. Li let his grades fall, and there was an economic recession at the time of the promise. Moreover, there was no definite detriment because Mr. Li's allegation of damage is not calculable; nor was there a substantial detriment because Mr. Li still gained valuable experience from working with the firm and he was not prevented from seeking employment elsewhere.

STATEMENT OF FACTS

Mr. Li wishes to bring a promissory estoppel claim against his former summer employer, Micheo & Yoon, for declining to fulfill its promise of employing him once he graduated law school. Mr. Li worked for Micheo & Yoon, a New Jersey-based top 100 law firm, during the summer after his first year of law school. Because of Mr. Li's impressive research and analytical skills and hardworking attitude, Janet Heinan, Director of Attorney Recruiting, told Mr. Li the firm would extend an offer of full-time employment to him in November of this third year in law school if he maintained a "high G.P.A.," was on journal or moot court, and worked for the firm during the summer after his second year in law school. Mr. Li was elated by the offer because he wished to work in "big law" and wanted to stay near his home state of Delaware.

Mr. Li accepted an offer from his law school's law review, worked for Micheo & Yoon his second summer, but decided to "relax" and allowed his G.P.A. to slip. At the time Ms. Heinan made the promise to Mr. Li, his G.P.A. was a 3.8; his second year G.P.A. dropped to a 3.5. The necessary G.P.A. to remain on the Dean's List at Mr. Li's law school is a 3.45. Even though there were opportunities for Mr. Li to interview with other firms, he elected not to do so because he relied on Ms. Heinan's statement.

At the time Ms. Heinan made the promise to extend an offer of employment to Mr. Li for two years in the future, there was a moderate economic recession. In October of Mr. Li's third year in law school, Ms. Heinan reached out to inform Mr. Li that the firm would no longer be able to hire him due to economic circumstances. The ongoing economic recession reduced the number of available jobs in the legal field, so Mr. Li could not find a position with another large law firm. He ultimately found employment with a solo practitioner who paid him a salary that was slightly over 25 percent of the starting salary at Micheo & Yoon.

PROF'S TIPS

You are referring to a person, so use "who" not "that."

DISCUSSION

I. Mr. Li cannot support a prima facie claim of promissory estoppel against the law firm because although the law firm made a definite promise with an expectation Mr. Li would rely on that promise, his reliance on that promise was not reasonable, and his detriment was neither definite nor substantial.

Spencer Li is bringing a promissory estoppel claim against his former employer, Micheo & Yoon, for reneging on its promise to hire him full-time after he graduated from law school. Promissory estoppel is a remedy by which a promisee may seek redress when a promisor should reasonably expect his promise to induce forbearance or action on the part of the promisee, limited to when injustice can only be avoided by the enforcement of the promise. RESTATEMENT (SECOND) OF CONTRACTS § 139(1) (Am. Law Inst. 1981). Promissory estoppel is applicable to *in futuro* promises where the promisor intends to abandon the promise, or where the promise is intended to influence another into action or forbearance of a legal right. *See Friedman v. Tappan Dev. Corp.*, 126 A.2d 646, 653 (N.J. 1956).

> **PROF'S TIPS**
> Italicize Latin terms unless they are fully part of the common legal vernacular. If you are not sure whether a term is a common one, look it up in a legal dictionary to see whether it is italicized.

In New Jersey, promissory estoppel requires: (1) the promisor made a definite promise; (2) the promisor made the promise expecting it to induce reliance by the promisee; (3) the promisee in fact reasonably relied on the promise; and (4) the promisee suffered a definite and substantial detriment because of reliance on the promise. *Malaker Corp. Stockholders Protective Comm. v. First Jersey Nat'l Bank*, 395 A.2d 222, 230 (N.J. Super. Ct. App. Div. 1978). The *sine qua non* for the applicability of promissory estoppel is the threshold element of a clear and definite promise. *Id.* at 230. Janet Heinan, the Director of Attorney Recruiting, told Mr. Li he would receive an offer from the firm if he met certain conditions, so there was a definite promise. That the Director of Attorney Recruiting made the promise and gave certain conditions to its fulfillment implies that Mr. Li was expected to rely on the promise. Therefore, at issue here is whether Mr. Li reasonably relied on this promise, and if so, whether this reliance forced Mr. Li to incur a definite and substantial detriment.

A. **Even though Mr. Li did rely on the law firm's promise, his reliance was not reasonable because: he failed to meet certain conditions of the promise, the time between when the promise was made and its expected performance was too long, and there were economic factors beyond the promisor's control.**

To satisfy the third element of a claim for promissory estoppel, a plaintiff must show that he reasonably relied on a representation made by the defendant, which induced him to abandon an existing right or influenced him to act or refrain from acting. *Friedman*, 126 A.2d at 653. The promissory estoppel approach applies to future promises and is a flexible doctrine. *Id.*; *Malaker*, 395 A.2d at 230. Because promissory estoppel rests on principles of fairness, courts typically treat the requirement of reasonable reliance as a question of fact reserved for the fact finder. *Friedman*, 126 A.2d at 646; RESTATEMENT OF CONTRACTS § 90.

When determining whether reliance on a promise is reasonable in a promissory estoppel claim, New Jersey courts look to several factors, including: the immediate circumstances surrounding the promise, the language of the promise, and external factors that could affect the reliability of the promise. *See Thomas v. Princeton Univ.*, No. A-0680-14T1, 2016 N.J. Super. Unpub. LEXIS 2515, at *1 (Super. Ct. App. Div. Nov. 23, 2016) (holding that a temporary employee's reliance on a promise of permanent employment was unreasonable, especially considering the promise was made two years prior); *Goldfarb v. Solimine*, No. A-3740-16T2, 2019 N.J. Super. LEXIS 1472, at *1, 28 (Super. Ct. App. Div. June 26, 2019) (holding that the plaintiff was reasonable in relying on a promise of employment because the job was to start immediately); *E. Orange Bd. of Educ. v. N.J. Sch. Const. Corp.*, 963 A.2d 865 (N.J. Super. Ct. App. Div. 2009) (holding that negative, external economic impacts can make it unreasonable to rely on a promise).

PROF'S TIPS

Note that "court" is not capitalized. Court is capitalized when it is part of a proper noun, the Supreme Court, or when you are submitting the document to the court in question, as in "This Court should affirm the …" (see the brief).

The court looks to the context—including the specific language and conditions—of the promise to determine whether it was reasonable to rely on the promise. *Malaker*, 395 A.2d at 230 (holding that there was no valid claim for promissory estoppel because a reasonable person would not rely on a promise with very few specifics discussed). The clearer and more specific the language and conditions in the promise, the more probable the plaintiff's reliance was reasonable and foreseeable, and the more likely injustice will result from refusing to enforce the agreement. *Peck v. Imedia, Inc.*, 679 A.2d 745, 752 (N.J. Super. Ct. App. Div. 1996); *Royal Assocs. v. Concannon*, 490 A.2d 357, 357 (N.J. Super. Ct. App. Div. 1985). When the promisee meets the conditions to receiving the benefit of a promise and the promisor takes actions that would lead a reasonable person to believe he would receive the benefit, the court may uphold reasonable reliance in a promissory estoppel claim. *Royal*, 490 A.2d at 359–60. For example, in *Royal*, a landlord had a no pets policy for his tenants, but he gave "special permission" to the plaintiffs to keep their dog so long as they controlled it. *Id.* After several years of allowing the pet to remain on the premises, the landlord attempted to force the plaintiffs to give up their dog. *Id.* The landlord admitted he had never seen the dog off a leash and that the plaintiffs complied with all conditions. *Id.* The tenant could likely have made alternative arrangements to live elsewhere or decided not to buy a pet, but did so in reliance on defendant's clear and definite promise that the tenant's dog would be allowed without trouble. *Id.* Because the plaintiffs met all the conditions of the promise and were allowed to bond with the dog for years, the court held that it was reasonable they relied on the landlord's promise that they could keep their dog. *Id.* at 362.

Conversely, where the conditions of the promise are clear, but the plaintiff fails to meet them, the court will not find reasonable reliance. *Bonczek v. Carter-Wallace, Inc.*, 701 A.2d 742, 744–46 (N.J. Super. Ct. App. Div. 1997). In *Bonczek*, the plaintiff was offered employment contingent upon the completion of reference checks establishing a generally positive character. *Id.* at 744. The plaintiff embellished his title and salary with his previous employer, which raised concerns about his credibility. *Id.* at 744–45. The court held that because the promise was contingent on specific conditions that the plaintiff did not meet, there was no valid promissory estoppel claim. *Id.* at 746.

When the factors leading to the promisor breaking the promise are within the promisor's control, it may be reasonable to rely on the promise. *Pop's Cones, Inc. v. Resorts Intern. Hotel, Inc.*, 704 A.2d 1321, 1326 (N.J. Super. Ct. App. Div. 1998); *see also Peck*, 679 A.2d at 745 (holding that an employee reasonably relied on an oral offer for a full-time position that was subsequently rescinded because the decision was based only on the employer's change of mind about the employee's fit). For example, in *Pop's Cones*, a casino induced a store owner to give up her lease at her current location to relocate to the casino. 704 A.2d at 1326. The store owner repeatedly told the casino the time by which she needed to renew her current lease. *Id.* at 1322. The casino told the store owner not to renew her lease and to "pack up ... and plan on moving." *Id.* Because virtually nothing remained to be determined by the parties, the casino told the store owner to "pack up," and it was at the casino's sole discretion to back out of the promise, the court held that there was a valid claim of promissory estoppel and it was reasonable for the store owner to rely on the promise. *Id.* at 1326.

When the promise is made in an indefinite situation, such as when the expected performance is remote in time or when the promise is made under uncertain economic circumstances, it is not reasonable to rely on the promise. *See Thomas*, 2016 N.J. Super. Unpub. LEXIS 2515 at *10 (holding that a term employee was not reasonable in relying on a promise of permanent employment due to his temporary status and because the promise was made two years before he was fired); *see also E. Orange*, 963 A.2d at 874–75 (holding that it was not reasonable for a school board to rely on state funds for school construction projects amid statewide budget cuts). If the timing of the promise is remote in nature from when the promise should come to fruition, and the promisee's relationship with the promisor is ephemeral, it may not be reasonable to rely on such a promise. *Id.* In *Thomas*, a term employee was promised a permanent position with his employer once his current construction project was complete. *Id.* These promises continued for two years while the employee continued his project and passed up opportunities to apply for permanent positions. *Id.* The court held it would not be reasonable to rely on the employer's promises given the conditions surrounding the promise—namely, the employee's term status and the elapsed time from the date of the original promise. *Id.* In contrast, where the promise is set to mature immediately, it is reasonable to rely on a promise. *Goldfarb*, N.J. Super. LEXIS 1472, at *1, **6–7. For example, in *Goldfarb*, the defendant promised the plaintiff a job managing his and his family's assets, where the plaintiff would receive a sizeable salary and a portion of investment gains. *Id.* at *1. The employment was to begin immediately, and the defendant promised to memorialize the agreement in writing. *Id.* at *1, *23. Given these definite circumstances, the court held that it was reasonable to rely on the defendant's promise of employment. *Id.* at *31.

When economic circumstances affect the viability of a promise, it is not reasonable to rely on promises. *See E. Orange*, 963 A.2d at 874–75; *see also Thomas*, 2016 N.J. Super. Unpub. LEXIS 2515 at *9. For instance, in *E. Orange*, a school board sought to compel New Jersey Schools Construction Corporation (SCC) to proceed with certain school construction projects that were delayed because of statewide budget cuts. 963 A.2d at 866–67. The SCC was responsible for distributing the funds for similar projects at public schools around the state. *Id.* at 867. Prior to the suit, the SCC determined that it would not be able to fund all of the projects due to a lack of funds. *Id.* Even though the school board previously received approval for their projects and was on the original priority list, its projects were cut in the reprioritization. *Id.* at 870. The court held that it was not reasonable for the school board to rely on the approval of their proposed projects given that no specific project was approved, especially in light of the dire funding issue. *Id.* Similarly, in *Thomas*, budget cuts impeded a university from fulfilling its promise to hire a term construction employee as a permanent employee. 2016 N.J. Super. Unpub. LEXIS 2515 at **3–4. Because of the budgetary cutbacks, the university had fewer projects available, which meant there was not enough revenue to pay employees. *Id.* at *6. Because the university had legitimate business reasons to forgo hiring the term employee—specifically budget cutbacks—the court held that it was not reasonable for the employee to rely on the university's promise made before the cutbacks. *Id.* at *9.

Mr. Li likely cannot support a claim of promissory estoppel because it was not reasonable for Mr. Li to rely on Micheo & Yoon's promise of future employment if he did not meet the law firm's conditions to Mr. Li's post-graduation employment. Ms. Heinan specifically told Mr. Li that he had to keep up a "high G.P.A." in order to receive an offer in his last year of law school. Mr. Li had a G.P.A. of 3.8 at the time Ms. Heinan made the promise, but he purposefully decided to "relax" his work ethic and allowed his G.P.A to drop to a 3.5. When the promisee does not satisfy the conditions of the promise, the court is unlikely to hold that reliance on the promise is reasonable. *Bonczek*, 701 A.2d at 744.

PROF'S TIPS

When you proofread your memorandum, glance at the Analysis sections to see whether there are underlines or italics—whichever you chose for case citation. If you see large stretches without either, it may mean that you are not using cases to support your assertions. That would be a problem since much of Analysis is about comparing and contrasting the facts of your case to the fact-based holding and rationale to precedent.

Like in *Bonczek*, *id.*, where the plaintiff failed to establish promissory estoppel when he failed to meet the employment's condition that he receive positive references, Mr. Li's employment was conditioned, in part, on a high G.P.A. While Mr. Li's 3.5 G.P.A is slightly above the 3.45 G.P.A. required to make the Dean's List, it is a G.P.A. that Micheo & Yoon and similarly ranked firm do not consider "high," thus Mr. Li has not met the condition of a "high G.P.A." Additionally, one of the reasons Micheo & Yoon hired Mr. Li was because of his hardworking attitude. If the firm viewed his relaxed attitude toward his schoolwork as an indication of how he would perform in the future, it might have reasonably concluded that Mr. Li was a bad fit for the firm.

Mr. Li could claim he met the conditions of the agreement. He was still on the Dean's List, he was on journal, and he worked for Micheo & Yoon during his second summer. In *Royal*, the court held that the tenants met the conditions of receiving the benefit of the landlord's promise because the landlord admitted they never broke the conditions, and he continuously allowed the tenants to have their dog for years. 490 A.2d at 359–60. While a 3.5 G.P.A. still allows a student to be on the Dean's List, the law firm's condition of a "high G.P.A." is more nebulous than the specific condition of keeping a dog on a leash and at the firm's discretion. Unlike in *Royal*, *id.* at 360, where the landlord gave the tenants special permission to not comply with the building's no pet policy, Mr. Li never discussed his G.P.A. with Micheo & Yoon. Because Mr. Li let his grades drop and the condition of a high G.P.A. would likely be defined by the law firm's prior policy, a court likely would not consider Mr. Li's reliance reasonable.

It was not reasonable for Mr. Li to rely on Micheo & Yoon's promise of employment because the promise was made too distant in time from its expected fulfillment. Ms. Heinan made the promise to employ Mr. Li almost two years before Mr. Li would be able to take the position. In *Thomas*, the court held that a term employee who relied on his employer's promise that he would become a permanent employee two years before being terminated did not rely reasonably because the promise was too far removed from the date of maturation. 2016 N.J. Super. Unpub. LEXIS 2515 at *10. Like the temporary nature of the term employee, *id.*, Mr. Li was a summer associate at the time of the law firm's promise, meaning that he was only a temporary employee. Mr. Li was also promised employment for a remote time in the future. In *Goldfarb*, the court found reasonable reliance where the plaintiff was also promised employment, but the promise was for an immediate position with the defendant. 2019 N.J. Super. LEXIS 1472 at **6–7. Conversely, Mr. Li was not expected to start until he graduated from law school two years later. In addition, the defendant in *Goldfarb* was promised that the agreement would be put into writing, *id.*, whereas Ms. Heinan only mentioned extending such an offer at a distant point in the future.

The external economic forces that affected the law firm's ability to deliver on its promise were likely such that it was unreasonable for Mr. Li to rely on the promise of employment. At the time Ms. Heinan made the statement regarding possible future employment to Mr. Li, there was a moderate economic recession. When Ms. Heinan informed Mr. Li that the firm could no longer employ him, many firms were also experiencing a decrease in job availability due to the dip in the economy. In *E. Orange*, statewide funding cuts led to the SCC defunding certain school projects. 963 A.2d at 874–75. In light of the dire funding issues for school projects across the state, it was not reasonable for the school's board to rely on promises that it would receive funding for their projects. *Id.* at 870. Similarly, Micheo & Yoon was likely affected by the negative effects that a recession can have on businesses nationwide. Ms. Heinan told Mr. Li the firm would be unable to hire him due to economic circumstances. In *Thomas*, the court held that when there are viable business reasons for not hiring someone and budgetary cutbacks, it is not reasonable to rely on a promise of employment. 2016 N.J. Super. Unpub. LEXIS 2515 at *9. The employer in *Thomas* had no new construction projects that would supply the funds necessary to hire new permanent employees. *Id.* at *4. Just as there needs to be funds to hire construction workers, a law firm would need the economic conditions to hire new lawyers. In the context of a slowing economy, which was evident at the time Ms. Heinan made the promise to Mr. Li, it would likely not be reasonable to rely on such a promise. Unlike the defendant in Pop's Cones, 704 A.2d at 1326, who was in complete control of the circumstances surrounding its promise, and in fact encouraged the plaintiff to continue to rely on his promises, an economic recession is not in the control of a law firm, and no one at the law firm explicitly continued to encourage Mr. Li to stay with the firm.

Because Mr. Li may not have met the conditions of the promise, was offered employment two years before he could take the position, and there were negative economic factors beyond the law firm's control impacting its ability to hire Mr. Li, the court will likely hold that it was not reasonable for Mr. Li to rely on Ms. Heinan's promise of employment.

B. **Mr. Li did not incur a definite and substantial detriment by relying on Micheo & Yoon's promise because any detriment is too speculative, and Mr. Li received some benefit from working with the law firm.**

An essential justification for the theory of promissory estoppel is avoiding substantial hardship or injustice stemming from the broken promise; therefore, the promisee must suffer some detriment in reliance on the promise. *Malaker*, 395 A.2d at 232. In New Jersey, there are two essential components that must be present to establish the element of detrimental reliance: (1) a definite detriment and (2) a substantial detriment. *Id.*, 395 A.2d at 232 (holding that a detriment must be substantial in nature); *Sadej v. Arturi*, No. A-1424-16T1, 2019 N.J. Super. Unpub. LEXIS 1043 at *1, *22 (Super. Ct. App. Div. May 7, 2019) (holding that a detriment must be definite and substantial); *Toll Bros., Inc. v. Bd. of Chosen Freeholders of Burlington*, 944 A.2d at **1, **19 (N.J. 2008) (holding that there must be definite and substantial detriment for a viable promissory estoppel claim).

If there is a clear way to calculate lost earnings as a result of relying on a promise, the detriment is definite. *Goldfarb*, 2019 N.J. Super. LEXIS 1472 at *1, 29–30 (Super. Ct. App. Div. June 26, 2019). In *Goldfarb*, the plaintiff was promised employment with the defendant to handle the defendant's assets. *Id.* at 1. In reliance on the defendant's promises, the plaintiff quit his current job, but the defendant withdrew the offer before the plaintiff could start. *Id.* The plaintiff was able to prove what his salary was for several years prior to quitting his job and showed that once he found a new job it was much less than he made previously and what he was promised by the defendant. *Id.* at *2, *26. Because the plaintiff was able to point to specific financial losses based on his changed employment in reliance on the defendant's promise, the court held there was a definite detriment that would allow a promissory estoppel claim. *Id.* at 30.

Definite detriment requires the damages the promisee purports to have suffered to be more than merely speculative. *Village Square Madison Ave., LLC v. TD Bank*, N.A., 2016 N.J. Super. Unpub. LEXIS 269 at *24. For example, in *Village Square*, the defendant pulled out of an agreement to obtain zoning and develop a property with Village Square, causing Village Square to incur costs in reliance on developing the area. *Id.* at *19–20. The plaintiff failed to show that the defendant was not diligent in pursuing the agreement because the defendant spent two years attempting to obtain zoning approval and it became clear it would not be able to obtain approval. *Id.* at 22. The court held that Village Square's assertions that it could have reaped financial gain from the sale of the property had it not relied on the defendant's promises to work together, were too speculative to constitute a definite detriment. *Id.* at 24.

Where a promisee is prevented from obtaining all or most of the benefit of a promise, the court is likely to find a substantial detriment. *Onorato Const., Inc. v. Eastman Const. Co.*, 711 A.2d 1363 (N.J. Super. Ct. App. Div. 1998); *see also King James Care Ctr. of Chatham 415 S. Blvd. Chatham v. Richardson*, 2018 N.J. Super. Unpub. LEXIS 4394 at *25–26 (holding that where the daughter of a nursing home resident neglected to pay any of the outstanding balance, there was a substantial detriment). For example, in *Onorato*, the plaintiff and subcontractor told the general contractor that the subcontractor was in financial difficulties and the general contractor should either pay the plaintiff directly or issue a joint check. 711 A.2d at 1364. The general contractor acknowledged it would do so, sent a portion of the payment as a joint check, but then later sent the rest to the subcontractor alone, who was insolvent. *Id.* Because the general contractor knew of the issues, acknowledged them orally and in writing, yet issued only one check as a joint payment, the court held that there was a substantial detriment. *Id.* at 1365–66. Likewise, when the promisee has no other option but to rely on the promisor's assertions, the court may find a substantial detriment. *King James*, 2018 N.J. Super. Unpub. LEXIS 4394 at *25–26. In *King James*, the daughter of a patient in a nursing home explicitly asserted that she was not personally liable for her mother's payments to the nursing home. *Id.* at *3. However, she had power of attorney over her mother and previously assured the nursing home that she would "promptly" fill out the necessary Medicaid paperwork and would pay for the remaining balance of her mother's care from her mother's assets. *Id.* at *3, *5. The court held that because the daughter allowed two years of payments to accrue while assuring the nursing home she would be responsible for the payments if Medicaid did not pay them, the nursing home incurred a substantial detriment for which the daughter was responsible. *Id.* at *25–26.

The non-exercise of a right to seek opportunity elsewhere is not a substantial detriment that supports a claim of detrimental reliance. *Malaker*, 395 A.2d at 232; *see also Friedman*, 126 A.2d at 652 (holding that where the plaintiff held land to be sold at a special price to a buyer, but the buyer later backed out, there was no detriment because the seller expended nothing and could still sell to someone else). For instance, in *Malaker*, a corporation's stockholder committee sued a bank alleging the bank made an oral promise to loan the corporation money, which it failed to do. 395 A.2d at 224. The corporation alleged it could have received funds elsewhere had it not relied on the bank's promise. *Id.* at 232. However, the court held there was no proof the corporation could have been successful in seeking loans elsewhere. *Id.* Ultimately, the court held the forbearance from seeking funding from other sources in reliance on the bank's promise to supply a loan was not sufficiently substantial to show detriment. *Id.*

Moreover, where the promisee receives most of the benefits of a promise, there is likely no substantial detriment. *Sadej*, 2019 N.J. Super. Unpub. LEXIS 1043 at *22. For instance, the plaintiffs in *Sadej* received zoning permits to make improvements to their home. *Id.* at *2. When they completed about 80 percent of the work, the city issued a stop order, saying the improvements did not comply with the permits. *Id.* The couple still completed most of the improvements (except for attaching their detached garage), was only held up for seven days, and received income from renting out the property. *Id.* at *23–24. Because the delay was minimal and the majority of projects were still completed, the court determined there was no substantial detriment. *Id.*

Mr. Li likely cannot establish that he suffered a definite detriment as a result of Micheo & Yoon's promise because his alleged damages are speculative as there is no way to calculate the exact damages Mr. Li incurred. In fact, the law firm could argue Mr. Li gained some benefit as a result of his experience with a top 100 law firm and the ability to stay in his home state during his summer associateships. For two years, Micheo & Yoon was diligent in giving Mr. Li "big law" experience. The alleged detriment in this case is similar to that in *Village Square*, where the plaintiff could not establish that it could have achieved financial gain had he exercised alternative options because there was no way to establish what Village Square earned through alternatives to working with the defendant. 2016 N.J. Super. Unpub. LEXIS 269. Analogously, Mr. Li did not apply to any other law firm positions, so there is no way to prove he could have acquired a legal job of the same caliber and salary as Micheo & Yoon had he never relied on Ms. Heinan's promise and worked for the law firm over his second summer.

Mr. Li could try to establish a definite method to calculate his lost earnings by comparing the salary he would have made with Micheo & Yoon to his current salary. Mr. Li's salary with a solo practitioner is seventy-five percent less than the starting salary at Micheo & Yoon. When there is a clear way to prove economic loss, the court may find there is a definite detriment. *Goldfarb*, 2019 N.J. Super. LEXIS 1472 at *1, *29–30. In *Goldfarb*, the plaintiff used past earnings to establish a definite loss when he quit his job in reliance on the defendant's promise of employment. *Id.* However, unlike in *Goldfarb*, *id.* at *30, where the plaintiff could point to specific loss, Mr. Li had no past earnings and did not forgo current employment, so he did not give up a definite salary to work with Micheo & Yoon.

Just as there is no definite detriment, Mr. Li also did not suffer a substantial detriment because Mr. Li was not prevented from seeking opportunities with other law firms. While Mr. Li was told he would receive an offer if he continued to work with Micheo & Yoon, the law firm never dissuaded Mr. Li from applying to other firms. Indeed, Mr. Li himself elected not to interview with other firms. Using forgoing potential opportunities as the way to establish detrimental reliance is too speculative to establish a substantial detriment. *Malaker*, 395 A.2d at 232. Just as in *Malaker*, *id.* at 232, where the court held forgoing alternative funding prospects in reliance on the bank's promise was too speculative to be substantial, when Mr. Li failed to seek alternative employment, he precluded any opportunity to determine whether he would have received another job offer from a top law firm, and how much he would have made there.

Moreover, that Mr. Li likely obtained a benefit from the experience of working at a prestigious law firm at Micheo & Yoon minimizes the likelihood that a court would find a substantial detriment. Mr. Li's experience strengthened his marketability and may have contributed to his ability to find a job in an uncertain job market. In *Sadej*, the court held that because the promisee received most of the value of the promise, there was no substantial detriment. 2019 N.J. Super. Unpub. LEXIS 1043 at *23–34. Here, the value Mr. Li received in continuing to work for

Micheo & Yoon outweighed any detriment he may have incurred in relying on its promise of post-graduation employment.

Mr. Li cannot likely establish that Micheo & Yoon's broken promise of future employment incurred definite or substantial detriment because Mr. Li did not lose any assured income, it would be too speculative to calculate potential lost earnings, and Micheo & Yoon did not prevent Mr. Li from seeking alternative employment opportunities at any time.

CONCLUSION

Under New Jersey law, Mr. Li will have difficulty establishing a prima facie claim of promissory estoppel because he did not reasonably rely on Micheo & Yoon's promise to employ him after he graduated because the promise was made too remote in time from when it could be fulfilled, it is possible Mr. Li did not meet the conditions of the promise, and external economic pressures affected the law firm's ability to fulfill its promise to Mr. Li. Likewise, Mr. Li cannot establish the essential factors of a definite and substantial detriment because Mr. Li's lost potential earnings are mere speculation and it was his choice to forgo other employment prospects.

Common Errors Editing Exercise

Can you spot (and not make) the common errors? Answers appear after the prompts.

1. Based on the law/facts/precedent, Li's actions would probably lose the promissory estoppel claim.
2. To determine whether or not the claim has merit, the plaintiff must....
3. Firstly, the plaintiff must establish ...; secondly, the plaintiff must show ...; and thirdly, ...
4. In that case, the Court held....
5. I will show that the plaintiff could've relied on....
6. The judgement in that case....
7. The defendant was given permission to use the property.
8. Micheo is likely to be found guilty of promissory estoppel.
9. The court may argue that Mr. Li was reasonable to rely on Ms. Heinan's assurance that.... That is because the court felt.... Also, the court disagreed with....
10. There is no promissory estoppel statue in New Jersey; instead, the courts rely on....
11. If a defendant exceeds the scope of consent, they may be found liable for trespass.
12. When Micheo & Yoon made the promise, they were essentially....

13. Courts have held that where a promisee is prevented from obtaining all or most of the benefit of a promise, the court is likely to find a substantial detriment. *Onorato Const., Inc. v. Eastman Const. Co.*, 711 A.2d 1363 (N.J. Super. Ct. App. Div. 1998).
14. It can be shown that Mr. Li was reasonable to rely on Micheo & Yoon's assurance that he would have a job after graduating law school.
15. Based on precedent/facts/the law, a court is unlikely to hold Micheo & Yoon liable for promissory estoppel.
16. A page-long paragraph.

Answers to the Common Errors Editing Exercise

1. You do not need to write that your conclusion is based on the law, facts, precedent, etc. What else would the basis be?
2. "Whether" is sufficient; there is no need for the "or not."
3. Aaaaargh! First, second, and third.
4. Do not capitalize "court" unless it's part of a proper name, the Supreme Court, or you are saying "this Court" because it is the court to which you are submitting the legal document.
5. There is no "I" or "me" in your legal document; a legal document does not really "show" anything, so use a different word; avoid contractions.
6. There is no "e" in judgment.
7. Be aware of passive voice! Do not say "was given permission"; rather, say "got permission" or something similar with only one verb. (The only time passive voice is occasionally appropriate is when used strategically in the Statement of Facts of an appellate brief; see Part II of this book.)
8. Your job is not to predict the final outcome of the case; it is to assess the viability of a claim. Moreover, this case is civil, not criminal; at issue is liability and not guilt. Finally, check to see whether Micheo is an accepted abbreviation of the firm name.
9. When referring to a court's action or position, do not use terms like argue, feel, or disagree.

10. Remember, your spell check may not catch common typos for statute, trial, and public.
11. Do not use "they"; rather use "he" or "she." "They" is appropriate only when used intentionally as a gender-neutral pronoun, however, not all legal writing contexts have progressed to make this shift, so I advise you to check with your professor.
12. Micheo & Yoon is the name of a firm. Like a company or corporation, a firm is an "it," not a "they."
13. Eliminate "courts have held." If you use that phrase the reader may expect you to string cite a number of cases from more than one court.
14. "It can be shown" is passive voice; it is also superfluous. Start with "Mr. Li was reasonable...."
15. "Based on precedent/facts/the law" is not a necessary phrase to include. In legal writing, it is clear that the support for/against a position will be precedent/facts/the law, especially since you will be citing cases to support the position. Start with "A court is unlikely...."
16. Do not write page-long paragraphs. If a paragraph is too long, break it up into multiple paragraphs (where the division makes sense).

PART II

Persuasive Writing

(a.k.a. the Appellate Brief or Motion)

ELEVEN

The Big Picture Part Deux

This chapter is similar to Chapter 1 in that it provides the reader with the purpose and audience for the writing. It will distinguish persuasive from predictive writing and identify where the reader is likely to encounter persuasive writing in the litigation process.

TWELVE

Theory of the Case and Standard of Review

This chapter will define the theory of the case and the standard of review; it will also illustrate their importance as the framework of an appellate brief.

THIRTEEN

Statement of the Issue(s)

This chapter will briefly discuss the Statement of the Issues and demonstrate through text and examples the distinction between a Statement of the Issues in a memorandum versus an appellate brief.

FOURTEEN

Summary of the Argument

This chapter will compare and contrast the Summary of the Argument in a brief to the Brief Answers in a memorandum. This section is particularly important because most legal writing books do not clearly describe how to write this section of an appellate brief.

FIFTEEN

Point Headings

This chapter will address major point headings and subheadings.

SIXTEEN

CREACC Revisited

This chapter will focus on writing the elements of CREACC persuasively.

SEVENTEEN

Statement of Facts

This chapter discusses a persuasive Statement of Facts and how it differs from a predictive one.

EIGHTEEN

Writing a Motion

This chapter demonstrates how to use the lessons from Part II of this book to write a motion. It includes a sample motion.

NINETEEN

Tips for Oral Argument

This chapter provides tips for using your writing as a foundation for a strong oral argument.

ELEVEN

The Big Picture Part Deux

In the second semester of a legal writing course, students traditionally write and argue an appellate brief. Just as I stated in Part I, you must begin the writing process by considering your audience. When you wrote your memorandum, you were writing for a reader who needed an impartial rendering of the strengths and weaknesses of a legal position. As a writer, you had no agenda but to present the law as it applied to a fact pattern and make predictions on that basis. Now, your charge is very different. When writing a persuasive document, your style of writing shifts. You are highlighting the facts and law that support your argument, and skillfully minimizing the impact of negative facts and law. This section of the book will provide you with tools to assist you in that process.

Notably, the appellate brief appears much later in the litigation timeline than the office memorandum (see the federal litigation timeline in the following section). By this time, the case has likely gone to summary judgment or to trial. In any event, there had to have been some judgment from which the appellant is appealing. The party who is appealing is called the appellant or petitioner, while the party arguing in favor of the judgment is the appellee or respondent. Whatever your use of party label, remain consistent—appellants argue against appellees and petitioners argue against respondents, never appellants against respondents or petitioners against appellees.

FEDERAL CIVIL LITIGATION TIMELINE

1. Event giving rise to claim
2. Client interview and necessary additional factual research
3. Legal research
4. Office memorandum
5. Client letter and decision whether to pursue claim
6. File and serve complaint
7. Answer to complaint
8. Discovery
9. Arbitration (possibly)
10. Pre-trial motions
11. Possible settlement
12. Trial
13. Verdict by jury or judgment by court
14. Possible notice of appeal

15 APPELLANT AND APPELLEE SUBMIT BRIEFS SPECIFIED IN SCHEDULING ORDER ⟵ **YOU ARE HERE**

16 Screening for oral argument by staff attorneys at the court of appeals

17 Oral argument

18 Panel of court of appeals deliberates and issues opinion and order

19 Either party may petition for a rehearing on *en banc* (heard by all the judges on the particular court)

20 *En banc* court of appeals may review brief and hear oral argument

21 *En banc* court of appeals issues opinion and order

22 Either party may appeal to the U.S. Supreme Court

23 Parties submit briefs and argue before the Court

24 The Court issues opinion and order

The chapters that ensue will focus on the differences in writing an appellate brief rather than a memorandum within the CREACC structure I addressed in the first section of this book; they will also address sections that appear in the brief that are not generally in an office memorandum. I do not address the macro-conclusion, which is a formal section in the appellate brief that is typically a single-sentence prayer for relief (see sample briefs for examples).

TWELVE

Standard of Review and Theory of the Case

Once you have your record (the documents related to the brief you will argue), use it to create a timeline of facts (see Chapter 17 for sample timelines). You may want to create two timelines—one for the facts of the case and another for the procedural history. Use the issues certified for appeal to do preliminary research so that you have a bit of legal context for initially identifying legally relevant facts. Not every fact is ultimately legally relevant; you may find yourself adding and removing facts from your timeline as you research the law. However, the timeline is a good first step because it assists you in organizing information vital to your case.

After you review your timeline, you will determine the standard of review and develop an initial theory of the case. Students often underestimate the critical importance of the standard of review and the theory of the case, but they are both critical components of a strong appellate brief.

Standard of Review

The standard of review is the lens through which the brief writer is asserting the appellate judge or judges should regard the case; it determines the amount of deference the appellate court will afford the lower court's decision. Accordingly, the standard of review the appellate court adopts can mean the appellant or petitioner will likely face an uphill battle or a tabula rasa. Consequently, both the appellant and appellee have a vested interest in the standard of review the court applies. Sometimes the standard of review is clear on its face, but if there is any grey area, the ability of the brief writer to convince the court of the appropriate level of deference to the lower court's decision is key.

In law school classes and moot court competitions, students are typically introduced to three standards of review: clearly erroneous, abuse of discretion, and de novo.

Clearly Erroneous

The clearly erroneous standard of review is based on the assertion that the lower court made an error of fact and affords the least deference to the lower court's decision. This standard of review is the most difficult for the appellant because the appellate court is least likely to grant review where the appellant is asserting that there is a factual error. Why? Well, because the lower court was the forum for fact finding; it was during the lower court's proceedings that the judge or jury had the opportunity to question or challenge any factual presentations. A higher court typically has only a transcript of the proceedings. Naturally, an appellate court would be reluctant to challenge facts that went unresolved at the lower level, especially because the fact-finding court (jury or judge) actually had firsthand access to that information and had the opportunity to elicit and arbitrate the facts.

Abuse of Discretion

Of the three listed standards of review, abuse of discretion cases afford mid-level deference to the lower court's decision. This is an appeal based on the ground that the lower court abused its discretion in making what is typically a procedural decision. While the appellate court has more access to the information supporting the basis of the appeal than under the clearly erroneous standard, it may still defer to the lower court judge's discretion.

De Novo

Finally, the de novo standard of review requires no deference to the lower court's decision; indeed, the Latin term *de novo* dictates that the court review the case anew. The basis for the appellant's de novo claim of error is that the lower court erred in its decision based on a misinterpretation of the law or misapplied the law to the facts of the case. This standard of review puts the appellant and appellee on an even playing field. Thus, it is typically the standard of review that your professor or the moot court board selects to make the problem fair. However, in practice, the standard of review is not always clear and can be a point of contention.

Determine the Standard of Review

Look at the following and determine the standard of review for each scenario.

1. The basis of appeal is that the lower court erroneously determined that Mr. Li's law school G.P.A. was a 3.5 when it indeed remained a 3.8.
2. The basis of the appeal is that the lower court wrongly defined promise under New Jersey law.
3. The basis of the appeal is that the lower court erroneously admitted expert testimony on typical law student grade point averages at law firms comparable to Micheo & Yoon.
4. The basis of the appeal is that the lower court incorrectly determined that Mr. Li's expectations were unreasonable according to promissory estoppel doctrine in the state of New Jersey.

Answers on the next page.

Answers to Standard of Review Exercise

1. The standard of review is clearly erroneous. The appellant is asking the court to review an error of fact that was determined at the fact-finding level.
2. The standard of review is de novo. The basis of appeal is on a pure question of law; the appellant is arguing that the lower court wrongly interpreted the applicable law.
3. The standard of review is abuse of discretion. The appellant is appealing on the basis that the lower court made a procedural error in allowing evidence that should have been inadmissible.
4. The standard of review is again de novo. This time the basis of appeal is that although the lower court may have rightly interpreted the law, it incorrectly applied the law to the case at bar.

Theory of the Case

Developing a theory of the case early in the brief-writing process is critical to creating a persuasive framework for your legal argument. Unfortunately, both law students and novice lawyers often fail to adopt and embrace a theory of the case. The theory of the case is an abridged story that you want to tell on behalf of your client; it is the framework from which you advocate. You may get a sense of the theory of the case before you research the law, or you may need to do some preliminary research to find out how to create a theory that fits within the confines of the applicable law. You are not wed to your initial theory of the case; you can modify it as you strengthen your understanding of the law.

The following are a couple of mini-fact patterns to help you understand the theory of the case.

Fact Pattern 1

A freshman student pledging a fraternity has a history of depression and anxiety. On the final evening of pledging, he

> quits the process and threatens to tell the university administration that the fraternity was violating the university policies against hazing. After stating his intention, the pledge runs out of the fraternity house with the president of the fraternity following five minutes later. The next morning, the freshman is found dead at the bottom of a bridge.

If you are the prosecuting attorney, your theory may be that the president of the fraternity followed the freshman and pushed him over the bridge to prevent him from telling the administration about the alleged misdeeds of the fraternity members. If you are the defense attorney, your theory may be the pledging process stressed the freshman out to the point that he jumped off the bridge.

Fact Pattern 2

> Spouses are in the process of getting a divorce. The spouses met in law school a decade earlier, and both graduated with honors. After five years of practicing law, Spouse 1 stayed home to raise the children while Spouse 2 worked long hours at a law firm. Spouse 1 is now demanding alimony that will allow that spouse to continue not to work.

What is your theory of the case likely to be if you are representing Spouse 1? What about Spouse 2?

Now review the promissory estoppel fact pattern earlier in this book. What would your theory of the case be if you are representing Spencer Li? What would it be if you are representing Micheo & Yoon?

A reader should be able to read the respective briefs of the appellant and appellee and see the theory of the case interwoven in the arguments. Understanding and embracing a theory of the case is essential to persuasive appellate advocacy. When I read draft briefs for which I cannot figure out whom the student represents, I coach my students to strengthen the theory of the case until they convince themselves of the strength of their position; buying into the story you are selling is an important first step in writing a brief. The theory of the case should be the clear lens through which the reader views your client's legal argument.

END OF CHAPTER SUMMARY

- The standard of review is the basis of appellate review. Understanding the and applying the appropriate standard of review is especially important because the standard of review dictates the level of deference the appellate court grants the lower court's decision.
- The theory of the case is fundamental to the legal argument. It is the underlying story the writer creates to garner the reader's support for the writer's legal position. The theory of the case is the basis of the writer's legal position and is interwoven throughout the persuasive document.

THIRTEEN

Statement of the Issue(s)

The paradigms for a Statement of the Issue(s) section that I set out in Part I for the memorandum generally hold true with the Statement of the Issue(s) for the appellate brief. So where should a writer begin? The easiest place is by identifying the number of major issues; typically, the number of issues corresponds to the number of issues certified for appeal. Notably, there are a couple of significant differences between the Statement of Issues in a brief and the Question (or Issues) Presented in a legal memorandum. The first is that if the issue is not too complicated, I encourage my student writers to include a single sentence for each issue rather than use that alternative format of a fact paragraph followed by legal questions. Again, as per Bryan Garner's advice (see Chapter 2), the general rule should be to limit the length of the sentence to no more than seventy-five words. The second major distinction with respect to the Statement of the Issue(s) in a persuasive document is, of course, the persuasive tone. Many students initially struggle with writing an effec-

PROF'S TIPS

There is no bright line rule for when an issue can be condensed into a single sentence. Follow your professor's guidance until you get a feel for the complexity of the issue; you may also be guided by the requirements of the court to which you are submitting the brief. Generally, you should attempt the single-sentence question before adopting a different approach.

tive Statement of the Issue(s). Often the tone is objective or over the top in the attempt to persuade; others include content that is too broad or too narrow. Also, remember that in your Statement you are asking for the legal conclusion and providing facts and context to lead your reader to the answer.

The following are the Statements of the Issue from the student-written appellate briefs in this book. Note that they are drafted to set a persuasive tone and use facts to lead the reader to a specific conclusion.

Write This

Appellant:

Whether, under the requirements for a promissory estoppel claim, Mr. Li reasonably relied on Micheo & Yoon's job offer—which was contingent on the completion of several conditions that he satisfied—and whether he in fact shifted his position in detriment on the promise, which they subsequently refused to enforce.

Appellee:

Whether Mr. Li can establish he reasonably relied to his detriment on Micheo & Yoon's promise of future employment, even though Micheo & Yoon made a conditional promise two years before its intended performance, Mr. Li did not meet the conditions, and the promise was made during the start of an economic recession which worsened by the time of performance.

Not This

Whether Mr. Li can support his claim of promissory estoppel when he reasonably relied on Micheo & Yoon's promise of future employment to his detriment.

The above Statement of the Issue states a legal conclusion rather than persuasively setting out the legal question; the reader should be able to read the Statement of the Issue and determine who the writer represents. Instead of telling the reader that Mr. Li reasonably relied on the promise, the reader should use facts to support the conclusion and effectively ask whether there is reasonable reliance.

Not This Either

> Appellant:
>
> Whether Mr. Li can support a claim for promissory estoppel when Micheo & Yoon offered him a position and without warning clearly snatched away his opportunity along with his hopes and dreams.

The above statement is over the top with respect to its attempt to be persuasive. Avoid words like "clearly" and "obviously"; they draw attention to the fact that the information may not be supported. Indeed, when I see these unnecessary modifiers, they immediately bring out my inner devil's advocate. Is it really that clear? Would we be here on appeal if it were?

Even without the world "clearly," the language in the example above is still over the top. Persuade your reader through framing the supporting facts rather than by relying on your flair for creative writing.

One More to Avoid

> Appellant:
>
> Whether Mr. Li can support a claim for promissory estoppel at the close of his first-year summer internship, the Director of Attorney Recruiting at Micheo & Yoon, Janet Heinan, told Mr. Li that if he (1) maintained a "high G.P.A.," (2) was on journal or moot court, and (3) worked for the firm his second summer, the firm would extend Mr. Li an offer in November of his third year of law school knowing there was an economic recession, yet did not extend Mr. Li an offer after Mr. Li made law review, worked for Micheo & Yoon his second law school summer, and did not pursue other employment opportunities as a result of that promise and accordingly had to take a lower-paying job after graduating.

Whew; that Statement of the Issue included so many facts that I forgot the legal issue! Remember the general seventy-five-word limit? That sentence included 127 words! The length and unwieldy language certainly detract from the persuasiveness of the sentence, but the substance also fails to support its purpose by not clearly connecting the facts to the elements at issue.

END OF CHAPTER SUMMARY

- The Statement of the Issue(s) is an opportunity for the writer to frame the legal issues persuasively.
- The Statement of the Issue(s) should frame the legal issue with facts that will lead the reader to an answer that is favorable to the writer's position.

FOURTEEN

Statement of Facts

Just as in your memorandum, every fact you include in your Analysis section should appear in your Statement of Facts. The difference in the brief is that your Statement of Facts is persuasive, or at least should be. A reader should be able to read your Statement of Facts and, based on its organization, language, and tone, know who you represent.

PROF'S TIPS

At the least you should create a timeline and even a draft Statement of Facts before writing your Analysis; I am simply suggesting that similar to the approach you should take when writing your memorandum, to ensure that you include all facts legally relevant to your Analysis, you should complete the Statement of Facts in your brief after writing the Analysis.

Organization

You do not have to organize your Statement of Facts chronologically. Your Statement of Facts should begin with a focus on your client and the facts that will likely elicit sympathy for its position. By the time you bring in the facts related to the opposition, you should have already set the stage with your client as the protagonist on legal high ground.

You should also write conscious of your reader's attention span. Only if it makes sense organizationally, try to put your most compelling facts in the beginning and end of your Statement of Facts; the reader's attention is most likely to wane in the middle. This logic also holds true for organization at the paragraph level.

Detail

While you must include all legally relevant facts in your Statement of Facts, you do not have to afford the same level of detail to every fact. You should detail the facts that support your position and de-emphasize those that counter it. Quotations from your record are one of those details that can be particularly powerful.

Passive Voice

If you are not using passive voice strategically, get rid of it. The general rule in legal writing (or any other kind) is that we avoid the passive voice. Passive voice reduces accuracy, and lawyers need accuracy. However, there may be occasions in which you will intentionally use passive voice in a persuasive document. Why? To deflect or minimize attention on negative facts.

For example, if you were reading the following two sentences, you could easily determine through use of detail and the active or passive voice whether the writer represented the defendant or plaintiff.

> Sentence 1: The plaintiff's leg was broken as a result of the accident.
> Sentence 2: The defendant shattered the plaintiff's femur by crashing his car into her after racing through the stop sign.

Citation

Although you did not cite facts in the memorandum's Statement of Facts, you will cite the record in your Statement of Facts for the brief; the method of citation may vary, so follow your professor's instruction. You must also cite facts from the record in your Argument.

END OF CHAPTER SUMMARY

- The Statement of Facts in a persuasive legal document should include all legally relevant facts.
- It should be organized logically, but that does not necessarily mean chronologically.
- It may be that it works best for the focus to begin on the writer's client or the most favorable facts, but the document should not sacrifice coherence.

FIFTEEN

Summary of the Argument

Remember your Brief Answer(s) to the Question(s) Presented or Statement of the Issue(s) for a memorandum? There is no Brief Answer(s) section in the appellate brief. Instead, there is a Summary of the Argument that serves largely the same function, but with some significant differences. The Summary of the Argument is exactly what it suggests: it summarizes the major arguments of the brief.

> **PROF'S TIPS**
>
> Just as with the Brief Answer, there is no citation in the Summary of the Argument.

Begin your Summary of the Argument with a strong introductory statement that encompasses your theory of the case, followed by an overview of your legal position that includes any context necessary to understand your arguments. If there is an overarching rule, it should be part of this context. Table 1 provides examples from the student-written appellate briefs at the end of this part.

TABLE 1.

Appellant	Appellee
A law student should be able to rely on the clear promises of future employment with a law firm, particularly when it is reasonable and foreseeable that he will forgo other employment opportunities as a result. This situation falls squarely within the interests that the doctrine of promissory estoppel was created to protect. In New Jersey, in order to succeed on a claim for promissory estoppel, four elements must be satisfied: (1) a clear and definite promise, (2) made with the expectation that the promisee will rely upon it, and (3) reasonable reliance upon the promise, (4) which results in definite and substantial detriment. It is uncontested that Micheo & Yoon made a promise of conditional employment to Spencer Li, with the expectation that he would rely upon it. Mr. Li can successfully demonstrate that the other two elements have been met as well—he was reasonable in his reliance upon the promise, which resulted in detrimental reliance. It was reasonable for Mr. Li to rely on Micheo & Yoon's promise of employment because Mr. Li consulted industry standard to inform his decision to rely on the promise, met all the necessary conditions to the offer, and Micheo & Yoon maintained sole discretion over the promise, which was substantially certain to mature within several months.	Not all promises are enforceable; when a promisee fails to meet the conditions associated with the promise, he cannot reasonably expect a court to enforce it. Under New Jersey's application of the promissory estoppel doctrine, there must be clear and convincing evidence to force a promisor to fulfill a promise, limited to when there is no other means to avoid injustice. The plaintiff has the burden to prove all four elements of promissory estoppel in order to prevail: (1) the promisor made a definite promise; (2) the promisor made the promise expecting it to induce reliance by the promisee; (3) the promisee in fact reasonably relied on the promise; and (4) the promisee suffered a definite and substantial detriment because of reliance on the promise. While Janet Heinan did make a promise of conditional employment to the appellant, the United States District Court for the District of New Jersey correctly concluded that the appellant failed to establish a prima facie claim of promissory estoppel because his reliance was not reasonable, nor did he incur a detriment as contemplated by the doctrine.

Once you have set forth an introductory statement with your theory of the case and provided any necessary context for your argument, the remainder of the Summary of the Argument includes the applicable rule for each CREACC, and persuasively and briefly applies that rule to applicable facts. The Summary of the Arguments in this book's sample briefs provide additional examples.

END OF CHAPTER SUMMARY

- The Summary of the Argument is the persuasive equivalent of the Brief Answer in the memorandum.
- This section is organized by assertion and includes rule statements from the CREACC briefly and persuasively applied to the facts of the case.
- This section includes no citation.

SIXTEEN

Point Headings

Memoranda often include headings but do not generally necessitate point headings. However, I usually introduce them as part of teaching my students to write memoranda because they are a helpful organizing tool. Certainly, headings vary in a memo, and they can be phrases or full sentences; they do not have to include *point* headings. However, briefs *do* necessitate point headings.

A point heading is a single-sentence conclusion; the writer uses it to make a point, an assertion. Each issue that warrants a CREACC must have a point heading. That point heading serves as the first C—or Conclusion—for the CREACC. Since the point heading is the Conclusion, immediately following the point heading is the Rule.

> **PROF'S TIPS**
> Some professors require a conclusion after the point heading. I find it superfluous, but please follow your professor's instruction.

If there are sub-issues that warrant subheadings, the major point heading is a broad heading that gives the legal conclusion that encompasses the subheadings. If the major point heading is without subheadings, it includes the legal conclusion and the factual basis. Likewise, the subheadings include the legal conclusion and the factual basis. The examples below illustrate the distinctions.

PROF'S TIPS

This is a major point heading that encompasses reasonable reliance and detrimental reliance—the two elements of promissory estoppel at issue; because it is summarizing the subheadings below, it includes the broad legal conclusions and not their factual bases. Also note that these broad headings do not usually include the word "because."

I. Mr. Li's reliance on Micheo & Yoon's promise of post-graduation employment was reasonable and he did in fact suffer a definite and substantial detriment as a result of such reliance meaning; accordingly, Mr. Li can support a prima facie claim for promissory estoppel.

This section would include any applicable roadmap. The overarching rule for promissory estoppel would appear here. In this section, the writer would include the overarching rule for promissory estoppel and identify the elements the court has elected to review. If the standard of review does not appear in its own section, it likely will be included here. It may also include a persuasive sentence or two to fortify the writer's position on the issues.

PROF'S TIPS

Note that the point heading for the reasonable reliance sub-issue includes a factual basis along with the legal conclusion.

A. Mr. Li's reliance on Micheo & Yoon's offer was reasonable because he complied with industry standard, properly satisfied all of the conditions of the promise, and relied on the promisor who exercised full control and discretion over a promise that was substantially certain to mature.

The remainder of the CREACC, beginning with the Rule, goes here.

PROF'S TIPS

Like the subheading above, this conclusion includes the legal conclusion and its factual basis. If this were an independent point heading without a subheading, the content would be the same.

B. Mr. Li incurred a definite and substantial detriment in reliance on Micheo & Yoon's promise because he sacrificed many other viable opportunities with other firms, experienced a considerable reduction in expected salary, and incurred substantial moving and housing expenses.

The remainder of the CREACC beginning with the Rule goes here.

END OF CHAPTER SUMMARY

- A point heading is a single-sentence legal conclusion and its basis.
- If you are using point headings, they serve as the C in your CREACC.
- If your document has multiple issues (multiple CREACCs), there should be a major summarizing point heading before the subheadings, summarizing the subheadings that serve as the Conclusions for each CREACC.

SEVENTEEN

CREACC Revisited

This chapter explores how you can strengthen the persuasive impact of your appellate brief or motion within the CREACC structure. Just as in the memorandum, you will begin with the Rule; that section will lay the groundwork of your CREACC. Also, as in the memorandum, the rule Explanation uses case illustrations and other sources to both explain the Rule and to demonstrate how courts apply the Rule. For a review on how to organize a CREACC, please review the CREACC structure in Part I of the book.

Like in the predictive memorandum, in a persuasive legal document, you are again applying the CREACC structure. Unlike the memorandum, however, you are no longer writing to predict; you are now writing to persuade. As a writer, you should always think strategically about what will appeal most to your reader. Accordingly, you should incorporate persuasive techniques pervasively throughout the document, and not just in your argument: from the theory of the case, word choice, selection of case support, point headings, and macro-organization, to sentence-level organization. In other words, you should be thinking about the effect of the organization and content on your audience throughout the writing process. You are writing to a judge, so what is most important is the law itself. Your job is to convince the judge—or judges—that your side is or should be the most legally tenable. Along with the analogical reasoning you use while applying case law, policy may play a strong role.

While you may or may not have explored policy considerations in your memorandum, it should certainly find a place here.

The most effective persuasive technique you can incorporate is your use of the law. That includes the language of a statute and the common law as it is has evolved. Certainly, judges want their decisions to be consistent with previous decisions in their jurisdiction; that is why mandatory authority is critical. Persuasive authority can also be useful to supplement—never to contradict—your mandatory authority. Laws from other jurisdictions and secondary sources can provide powerful guidance to the judges reading your brief.

Balancing Your Factors

Sometimes the rule under which you will argue will be comprised of multiple factors; writing professors like to select brief problems that require the students to engage in prioritizing and balancing factors. It is a skill set we like to see students learn and incorporate in their writing. If a rule has multiple factors or considerations, in the rule Explanation the writer must walk the reader through how the courts balance factors and/or apply any existent balancing test. Certainly, looking to the opinions of the court to which you are appealing should provide guidance on how to argue the factors. After you have used case law to demonstrate how courts weigh factors and various considerations, you will balance those factors in your client's favor in your Analysis section.

How to Incorporate Policy

The case illustrations in your rule Explanation include the holdings that support your premises. However, a critical part of the case illustration is the rationale, or basis for the holding. Understanding and highlighting that rationale in the rule Explanation are essential to your Argument (***what was Analysis in your memorandum***) section. Part of the rationale may very well include policy, and specifically concepts based in (notions of) equity and justice. If the court highlighted the broader social implications of its decision, it could play a critical role in how you incorporate the holding in your argument.

The Analysis is called the Argument in a brief, and as in your memorandum, you will organize the Argument around assertions that follow the general organization of the premises in your rule Explanation. Although you will compare your facts to that of precedent, the Argument is where you will also make clear the policy implications of the decision the court is charged to make. These policy implications should appeal to the reader's sense of justice and equity, or even emotional appeal as appropriate.

A more extreme example of highlighting the broader social implications of a decision is a slippery slope argument; this is also sometimes referred to as the snowball effect. The writer signals to the reader that a decision in favor of the opposition could have a negative impact that extends beyond the confines of the case at bar. For example, using the promissory estoppel case in this book, a slippery slope argument could be that to hold in favor of Micheo & Yoon could undermine the long-standing good faith relationship between law students and law firms; or the appellee could argue that a decision in favor of Mr. Li could generate a chilling effect on law firms extending offers to law students.

Counter-Analysis in the Brief

A distinctive characteristic in your brief is the Counter-Analysis. In the memorandum, you are writing to an audience who needs to understand the strengths and weaknesses of the side you identify as strongest to fully prepare a legal strategy. That is why you will highlight your Counter-Analysis in a memorandum. To the contrary, in a persuasive document the last thing you want to do is highlight the weaknesses of your argument; nor do you want to make arguments that opposing counsel may overlook. Counter-Analysis in a brief may seem counterintuitive. Not all professors require students to include Counter-Analysis, but it is an effective way to minimize the impact of your opponent's stronger arguments, and it is wonderful preparation for oral argument.

So how then do you handle counter authority from your rule Explanation when writing your Argument? The key is distinction. In a memorandum you often include Counter-Analysis in a paragraph separate from the Analysis; in a brief, that is not the case. In a brief the Counter-Analysis of each assertion still follows the Analysis, but it does not typically appear in a paragraph to highlight it. Instead, the Counter-Analysis is where you will distinguish negative authority from the facts of your case.

Below is an excerpt from the appellee brief in this book. Note that in both examples, the writer de-emphasizes the Counter-Analysis by beginning it in the center of the paragraph rather than the beginning.

Example from Appellant's Brief

The logistics of Mr. Li's offer were sufficiently definite in nature, making it reasonable for him to rely on the offer maturing as expected. While the promise of employment may have initially been made two years in advance, the validity of the promise was reinforced when Mr. Li completed his second summer with Micheo & Yoon, where "his work was as outstanding as his first-year performance." R. 22. Given that law firm culture dictates that students who work at the firm during the second-year summer are typically extended offers to join the firm after graduation, the promise of employment extended to Mr. Li was effectively renewed going into his third year of law school, just months before he expected the formal offer to be made in November of his third year. Like the plaintiff in *Schley*, 2008 U.S. Dist. LEXIS 96059, at *13–14, who had negotiated most of the terms of his employment, purchased a home, and left his previous job, Mr. Li had negotiated the material terms of his employment, made living arrangements contingent on the offer, and forgone alternative employment opportunities. R. 12, 16, 22. While Mr. Li did not have to move cities, he was induced to make a down payment on a house in reliance on the firm's offer and gave up his prior apartment lease. R. 28. Mr. Li did so only because he was confident that he would have a stable job with the firm. He discussed these plans and asked for guidance from several of the associates at Micheo & Yoon who he had fostered connections with over his two summers. R. 28. Distinguishable from the

PROF'S TIPS

The word "distinguishable" is a good (and often preferable) word to use in signaling the transition to Counter-Analysis. If you find yourself using it frequently, use synonyms to change things up.

term employee in *Thomas*, 2016 N.J. Super. Unpub. LEXIS 2515 at *3–4, who relied unreasonably on a promise to potentially make an offer at some unspecified point in time, Mr. Li relied reasonably on an express promise to offer him employment in the near future, just months after he had fulfilled the third condition to the promise. R. 20, 22.

Example from Appellee's Brief

Mr. Li not only failed to meet the conditions of the law firm's promise, but the timing of the promise made it so that no reasonable person should have relied on it. It was not reasonable for Mr. Li to rely on Micheo & Yoon's promise of employment because the promise was made too distant in time from when it was to be fulfilled. Janet Heinan, the Director of Attorney Recruiting for Micheo & Yoon, made the promise to employ Mr. Li almost two years before Mr. Li would be able to take the position. R. 20. In *Thomas*, the court held a term employee who relied on his employer's promise to become a permanent employee two years before being terminated did not rely reasonably because the promise was too far removed from the date of maturation. 2016 N.J. Super. LEXIS 2515 at *10. Like the temporary nature of the term employee, *id.*, Mr. Li was a summer associate at the time of the law firm's promise, meaning he was only a temporary employee. R. 21. Unlike situations where the courts have found plaintiffs were reasonable in relying on a promise of immediate employment, *Schley*, 2008 U.S. Dist. LEXIS 96059 at *17, Mr. Li was also promised employment for a remote time in the future. The plaintiff in *Schley* was also promised employment, but he was found to have relied reasonably because he entered into extensive negotiations, signed a final offer, and was encouraged to move immediately after the negotiations were completed. *Id.* In contrast, Mr. Li was not supposed to start until two years later and never signed any written offer. R. 20.

A FEW ADDITIONAL TIPS FOR YOUR ARGUMENT

- The brief you write will likely be about a case on appeal from an Order Granting Summary Judgment. Remember that to win on summary judgment, the movant must establish that there is no dispute of material fact. Therefore, if you are writing on behalf of the party arguing for summary judgment, you cannot dispute the facts. To the extent there is a factual discrepancy, you must argue that your client wins irrespective of that discrepancy, otherwise the court will determine that the case should go to a fact finder; in other words, you lose! For example, if the appellee argues that Mr. Li was actually a worse student than he represented, the court may determine that it is an issue that should be reviewed by a fact finder. Accordingly, the appellee would lose because the case would be remanded to the lower court and the appellant would have its day in court.
- Can you pass the eye roll test? In an attempt to persuade, do not yield to the temptation to go overboard. Remember that you are writing a legal document, not a short story or a script for a telenovela. Avoid unnecessary modifiers like "extremely" or "very." The ones I most commonly see are "clearly" and "obviously." My thought is usually if it really is that clear or obvious, why is there a need for the argument?
- Try to avoid using the word "concede" (I will address this again in the chapter on oral argument). Use more equivocal words of exception such as "even if" or "although." If you must give up a point, follow it with a "however" to show that while your opponent may have the advantage on that point, your client still has the stronger position overall.

END OF CHAPTER SUMMARY

- Just as with the memorandum, you will incorporate the CREACC format.
- The persuasive writing in an appellate brief may require special attention to:
  - Balancing and weighing factors;
  - Effectively incorporating policy to support your legal argument; and
  - Using case distinction rather than pointing out counter-arguments.
- Avoid exaggeration and unnecessary modifiers.

EIGHTEEN

Writing a Motion

There exist a plethora of motions: motion to dismiss, motion for judgment on the pleadings, motion for summary judgment, to name a handful. Like the appellate brief, motions are written persuasively as you are asking the court to take an action that benefits your client. You will find that the same principles of persuasive writing necessary for a strong brief also hold true for a motion.

In a first-year legal writing class, motion for summary judgment is one of the more common persuasive writing assignments. On the litigation timeline, the defendant moves for summary judgment after the complaints, answers to the complaints, and discovery. Summary judgment is a pre-trial adjudication; many civil cases are decided on a summary judgment basis and never make it to trial unless there is a successful appeal.

Summary judgment is only available when the material facts (the facts on which the court would base its decision) are not in dispute. Because there is no genuine issue of material fact, there is no need for a jury or judge to serve as fact finder, and the judge may decide solely on the law as applied to the undisputed facts (i.e., evidence that can be used: admissions, sworn testimony, affidavits, interrogatories, or anything else executed under the penalty of perjury). Here, the judge is not deciding on the facts themselves, but rather on whether there is a dispute between the parties on those facts.

Both the plaintiff and the defendant can request summary judgment; indeed, most defendants move for summary judgment, and the plaintiffs often issue a cross-motion for summary judgment on the same pleadings even while arguing the merits of their own position.

Summary judgment can be total or partial (on some of the disputed legal issues). There are often several counts in a complaint, and the parties can argue for or against summary judgment based on those respective counts. Partial summary judgment means that, should the case go to trial, the counts on which the court granted summary judgment are not going to be litigated, but the rest will.

Each jurisdiction has its own standard for summary judgment, but the general concept is the same across jurisdictions. That standard requires that the party requesting it establish that in presenting the facts of the case in the light most favorable to the party not moving for summary judgment, there is no genuine dispute about the material facts. Accordingly, the writer must first establish that there are no issues of material fact in dispute before moving to discuss the legal merits of the case. The writer is to use the record obtained in discovery to cite facts, and this includes both written discovery and depositions.

A response disputing summary judgment will likely first argue that there are material facts in dispute. The party can also argue that discovery is incomplete and a decision on summary judgment is incomplete, although this is not likely to be a possible argument in a 1L writing assignment. More likely, if the material facts are not in dispute, the motion should argue that the moving party will not prevail on the merits of the argument.

The length of your motion will vary according to the rules of the jurisdiction, or for our purposes, your professor's page-length requirements. The following is a sample motion for summary judgment. Please keep in mind that it may vary somewhat from your professor's specifications, but it should give you a good sense of the persuasive style of writing you are expected to adopt.

Sample Motion for Summary Judgment

IN THE UNITED STATES DISTRICT COURT FOR
THE DISTRICT OF NEW JERSEY

SPENCER LI,
Plaintiff,

CASE NO.:

v.
MICHEO & YOON
Defendant

_______________________________/

DEFENDANT'S MOTION FOR SUMMARY JUDGMENT

COMES NOW Defendant, MICHEO & YOON, by and through the undersigned counsel, and hereby file this Motion for Summary Judgment pursuant to Rule 4:46 of the New Jersey Rules of Civil Procedure, and as grounds therefore states the following:

INTRODUCTION AND UNDISPUTED FACTS

1. Defendant, MICHEO & YOON, is a prestigious New Jersey law firm ranking 88th on AmFirm 100.
2. MICHEO & YOON hired Plaintiff, SPENCER LI, as a summer associate during his first year of law school.
3. Based on MR. LI's performance during his first summer, MICHEO & YOON offered MR. LI a conditional offer of full-time employment at the close of his first-year internship.
4. Director of Attorney Recruiting, JANET HEINAN, told MR. LI that if he maintained a high G.P.A., joined journal or moot court, and worked for the firm during his second summer, the firm would extend a formal offer of employment during the fall of MR. LI's third year of law school.
5. Prior to his second summer, MR. LI joined Law Review and allowed his G.P.A to drop from a 3.8 at the time of the conditional offer, to a 3.5 during his second year of law school. Such a drop in performance subsequently dropped his rank from the top 5 percent of students to only the top one-third of students.

6. MR. LI worked at MICHEO & YOON during his second summer, and his performance reviews indicated satisfactory work.

7. MR. LI elected not to interview with any other firms.

8. In October of his third year of law school, MS. HEINAN notified MR. LI that MICHEO & YOON would be unable to extend a formal offer due to unforeseen economic circumstances outside of its control, which impacted the entire industry.

9. MR. LI secured post-graduate employment with a solo practitioner in Delaware prior to his law school graduation. The cost of living in Delaware's largest city is 73 percent less than in New Jersey.

10. MR. LI currently works in Pennsylvania in a job that pays $100,000 per year. The cost of living in Pennsylvania is almost half what it is in New Jersey.

SUMMARY JUDGMENT STANDARD

Summary judgment is proper when after all legitimate inferences are drawn in the non-moving party's favor, there exists no genuine dispute of material fact and the moving party is entitled to judgment as a matter of law. N.J. Court Rules, R. 4:46-2(c). A genuine issue of material fact is established only if the evidence submitted by both parties, with inferences favoring the non-moving party, would require submission of the issue to a trier of fact. *Id.* The opposing party must do more than point to just *any* dispute in fact; rather they must point to a dispute in fact that is material or substantial to the case. *Brill v. Guardian Life Ins. Co. of Am.*, 142 N.J. 520, 529 (1995).

If a reasonable fact finder could decide in the non-moving party's favor, then the moving party has not demonstrated that it is entitled to judgment as a matter of law and the court must deny the movant's summary judgment motion. *Globe Motor Co. v. Igdalev*, 255 N.J. 469, 480 (2016). Even if there is the slightest doubt as to the presence or existence of an issue of material fact, the entry of summary judgment is prohibited, and adjudication must be reserved for the fact finder. *Akhtar v. JDN Props. at Florham Park, LLC*, 439 N.J. Super. 391, 399 (N.J. Super. App. Div. 2015). Similarly, any issues of credibility must be left to the fact finder. *Id.* Thus, summary judgment should be denied, unless "the right thereto appears so clearly as to leave no room for controversy." *Id.* (quoting *Saldana v. DiMedio*, 275 N.J. Super. 488, 495 (N.J. Super. App. Div. 1994)).

SUMMARY OF THE ARGUMENT

MICHEO & YOON is entitled to a grant of Summary Judgment against MR. LI's claims for the following reasons:

1. MR. LI's reliance on the conditional statement from MS. HEINAN and MICHEO & YOON was unreasonable because he actively failed to meet the conditions of the statement, there were no formal procedures followed, there was an external and uncontrollable economic recession that impacted employment opportunities at all law firms, and the temporal gap between the statement and the presumed time of employment was too great.
2. MR. LI did not experience a detriment in reliance on MICHEO & YOON's conditional offer because the alleged detriment is merely speculative, and even so is not substantial, as MR. LI was benefited by his previous employment with the firm, during his first and second summer of law school.

ARGUMENT

A. MR. LI's reliance on the conditional statement from MS. HEINAN and MICHEO & YOON was unreasonable due to his failure to fulfill the conditions and external and uncontrollable extenuating circumstances.

Where a plaintiff seeks to make a claim of promissory estoppel, they must make a showing of unambiguous, reasonable reliance on the promise, satisfying the third element of promissory estoppel. *West Morris Pediatrics, P.A. v. Henry Schein, Inc.*, 897 A.2d 1140, 1154 (N.J. Super. Law Div. 2004); *In re Phillips Petroleum Sec. Litig.*, 881 F.2d 1236, 1250 (3d Cir. 1989). It is well settled law that when the plaintiff has not fully satisfied all the conditions of the promise, the promise may not be reasonably relied upon. *Bonczek v. Carter-Wallace, Inc.*, 701 A.2d 742, 744–46 (N.J. Super. Ct. App. Div. 1997); *Wiegand v. Motiva Enters., LLC*, 295 F. Supp. 2d 465 (D.N.J. 2003) (holding that when an employee met conditions set out by his employer in order to maintain employment, the reliance was reasonable); *Massaro Ltd. P'ship (Park W. Two) v. Baker & Taylor Inc.*, 161 F. App'x 185 (3d Cir. 2005) (holding that reliance is not reasonable when a specific condition is not met). In *Bonczek*, an attorney was offered a position at a law firm conditioned upon the completion of reference checks that were "generally positive in content and character." 701 A.2d at 744. The law firm's reference checks raised questions regarding the accuracy of the attorney's representations of his job title and salary. *Id.* at 745. Upon the completion of the reference checks, the law firm opted to rescind the offer based on the attorney's misrepresentations. *Id.* The court ultimately held that it was unreasonable for the attorney to rely on the conditional job offer while simultaneously failing the conditioned reference checks due to his own misrepresentation. *Id.*

Even if the plaintiff satisfied all the conditions of the promise, courts look to numerous additional factors when determining whether reliance on a promise is reasonable, including the language, circumstances, timeline, and other factors external to the promise itself. *In re Phillips*, 881 F.2d at 1250 (holding that a mere expression of future intention cannot be reasonably relied upon); *Thomas v. Princeton Univ.*, No. A-0680-14T1, 2016 N.J. Super. Unpub. LEXIS 2515, at *1 (Super. Ct. App. Div. Nov. 23, 2016) (holding that a term employee was not reasonable in their reliance on representation that they may remain permanently employed at the end of the term due to the temporary nature of his employment and the representation being made two years in advance); *Shley v. Microsoft Corp.*, 2008 U.S. Dist. LEXIS 96059 (holding that where a promise is set to mature immediately, or in a practical time frame, reliance is reasonable).

A large temporal gap between the promise and the performance may not be reasonably relied upon, as the specific performance is too remote in time to know concretely the conditions will be satisfied, without external interference. *Thomas*, 2016 N.J. Super. LEXIS 2515 at *1. In *Thomas*, a university employee, working a temporary position as construction manager, expressed an interest in taking on a permanent role at the school, two years before his employment term was set to conclude. *Id.* at *3. His supervisor acknowledged his interest, promised future, permanent employment, and discouraged the employee from seeking other positions. *Id.* at *5. At the conclusion of the employee's term, and two years after his supervisor promised permanent employment, he was discharged from his position due to budgetary cutbacks. *Id.* at *6. Given the nature of his temporary employment, and the temporal gap between the promise and the expected performance, the court held that the employee was not reasonable in his reliance on the promise. *Id.* at *10.

Courts have recognized economic conditions as being an external factor, outside the promisor's control, that may fairly impact reasonability of reliance. *E. Orange Bd. of Educ. v. N.J. Sch. Const. Corp.*, 963 A.2d

865 (N.J. Super. Ct. App. Div. 2009). In *E. Orange*, a school board filed an action against the New Jersey Schools Construction Corporation (SCC) to compel advancement of school-related construction projects that were delayed due to statewide budgetary cutbacks. *Id.* at 866–67. Due to economic conditions, the SCC had to rescind prior project approvals and fund allocations, including those granted to the petitioning school board. *Id.* at 867. While the school board had previously approved funding, it made no argument or showing that its proposed projects were of a greater need to demand funding in light of the statewide budget cuts. *Id.* at 872–73. The court therefore held that the school board's reliance on a promise for state funds was not reasonable given the economic conditions at the time. *Id.*

Conversely, external factors that rest within the promisor's control may be reasonably relied upon. *Pop's Cones, Inc. v. Resorts Intern. Hotel, Inc.*, 704 A.2d 1321 (N.J. Super. Ct. App. Div. 1998); *Peck v. Imedia, Inc.*, 679 A.2d 745 (N.J. Super. Ct. App. Div. 1996) (holding there was reasonable reliance where an employer rescinded an offer of employment based solely on a change in heart regarding the prospective employee's character and social fitness). In *Pop's Cones*, a frozen yogurt franchisee entered into negotiations with a casino to relocate its operation to the casino's boardwalk property. 704 A.2d at 1322. In order to relocate, the store owner had to give up their current lease within a specified time, in reliance on the promise and encouragement from the casino. *Id.* The franchisee and casino engaged in a successful trial run with a frozen yogurt vending cart, to "test the traffic flow." *Id.* at 1322. The casino ultimately reneged on its offer, and the storeowner was forced to make last-minute arrangements as their prior location had already been re-let to another retailer. *Id.* at 1323. The court held that because the recission of the promise rested solely in control of the casino, it was reasonable for the franchisee to rely on its promise. *Id.* at 1326.

Mr. Li was unreasonable in his reliance on Micheo & Yoon's conditional offer of employment because he did not fully satisfy all the conditions of the offer, especially as it related to maintaining his high G.P.A. Ms. Heinan expressly included a condition that Mr. Li keep up a "high G.P.A." in the job offer. At the time the promise was made, Mr. Li held an impressive G.P.A. of 3.8, however, he actively allowed himself to relax in his studies, resulting in his G.P.A. dropping to 3.5. In *Bonczek*, an employee's failure to provide positive references resulted in a failure to satisfy the conditions of a promise for employment. 701 A.2d at 744. The determination of what constitutes a "positive reference" was an ambiguous one, and rested in the opinion of the employer, yet the court still held in favor of the employer, stating that the prospective employee failed to meet the conditions of the promise. *Id.* Likewise, the determination of what constitutes a "high" G.P.A. is an ambiguous one, as Mr. Li still remained on the Dean's List, even after his G.P.A. dropped. However, Micheo & Yoon, and other similarly situated and ranked firms, do not consider a 3.5 to be a "high" G.P.A. Thus, just as in *Bonczek*, *id.*, Mr. Li did not satisfy the conditions outlined by Ms. Heinan in her promise, making it unreasonable for Mr. Li to have relied on the promise.

The large temporal gap, between the time Ms. Heinan made the promise and the time the performance was expected, further makes reliance on the promise unreasonable. Ms. Heinan made the conditional offer nearly two years prior to Mr. Li's graduation and before he could actually be able to take the position. Mr. Li's case is virtually identical to the case in *Thomas*, where the court found that a temporary employee, employed for a fixed term, was not reasonable in relying on a promise for permanent employment made two years before his term concluded. 2016 N.J. Super. Unpub. LEXIS 2512 at *10. As a summer associate, Mr. Li was also a temporary employee, employed on a fixed term. The court held that the promise in *Thomas* was made too remote in time because it was made two years prior to the expected date of maturation. *Id.* Similarly, Ms. Heinan's conditional promise was also made nearly two years prior to the expected date when Mr. Li could begin the permanent role.

Moreover, Ms. Heinan's conditional promise was made during a period of economic instability in the form of a moderate recession, resting outside the control of Micheo & Yoon. The economic climate was a driving force, in addition to Mr. Li's failure to satisfy the conditions of the promise, in causing Micheo & Yoon to rescind its offer. In *E. Orange*, economic conditions forced a promisor to renege on its initial promise. 963 A.2d at 874. In that case, New Jersey was experiencing statewide budget cuts that left many school boards without funding for certain projects. *Id.* Given that the economic conditions were outside the control of the SCC, the court held that it was unreasonable for the school boards to rely on the SCC's promise, as the SCC had no control over the economy. *Id.* at 870. Similarly, Micheo & Yoon was not the only law firm to be negatively impacted by the recession; many other firms were experiencing the same hardship, causing a decrease in job availability and pay. Given that the dip in the economy was out of the control of Micheo & Yoon, and it was an industry-wide hardship, it was not reasonable for Mr. Li to rely on the conditional promise made by Ms. Heinan.

There were no factors, resting within the control of Micheo & Yoon, that subsequently caused the firm to rescind the conditional offer, even if all conditions of the promise were met. The decision to rescind the offer was a pragmatic one based off of the economy and Mr. Li's failure to satisfy the conditions. This can be distinguished from *Pop's Cones*, where the casino explicitly encouraged the franchisee to give up their current lease and then subsequently reneged on their promise. 704 A.2d at 1326. The decision to renege on the promise in *Pop's Cones* was made solely by the casino and was not due to any external, uncontrollable factors or the franchisee's conduct, and thus the court held that reliance was reasonable. *Id.* Conversely the factors leading to the decision by Micheo & Yoon to rescind the conditional offer initially given to Mr. Li were not in the complete control of the law firm, making reliance unreasonable.

Mr. Li was not reasonable in his reliance on the conditional offer for permanent, post-graduation employment from Micheo & Yoon. Not only did Mr. Li not fully satisfy all the conditions of the promise, conditions that were in his sole control, the temporal gap between the date of the promise and the date of the expected performance was too large for reliance to be reasonable. Furthermore, external economic forces made reliance even more unreasonable, as an economic recession caused an industry-wide decrease in job and salary availability. These economic factors were fully outside the control of Micheo & Yoon, and there were no factors that rested within the control of Micheo & Yoon that caused the promise to be rescinded. Therefore, Mr. Li was not reasonable in relying on Ms. Heinan's offer.

B. **MR. LI did not experience a definitive or substantial detriment in reliance on MICHEO & YOON's conditional offer, and instead, incurred a benefit due to his prior summer employment with the law firm.**

In bringing a claim for promissory estoppel, the plaintiff must show that they suffered some detriment in their reliance on the promise. *Malaker Corp. Stockholders Protective Committee v. First Jersey Nat'l Bank*, 395 A.2d 222, 230 (N.J. Super. Ct. App. Div. 1978). Such detriment must be both definite and substantial in order to satisfy the fourth element of promissory estoppel—detrimental reliance. *Id.*; *Toll Bros., Inc. v. Bd. of Chosen Freeholders of Burlington*, 944 A.2d at **1, **19 (N.J. 2008) (holding that the plaintiff must have suffered a definite and substantial detriment for a claim of promissory estoppel to survive).

The mere speculation of detriment is not enough to establish detrimental reliance, as it does not satisfy the "definite" element of detrimental reliance. *Village Square Madison Ave., LLC v. T.D. Bank*, N.A., 2016 N.J. Super. Unpub. LEXIS 269 at *24; *Malaker*, 395 A.2d at 227 (holding that a promise was unenforceable as a matter of law where no trier of fact could determine, without sheer speculation, that a bank complied or breached the promise). In *Village Square*, a bank backed out of an agreement to obtain zoning and develop the property with a real estate development company. 2016 N.J. Super. Unpub. LEXIS 269 at *20. The property developer subsequently brought an action for promissory estoppel against the bank, as the developer was forced to incur costs in reliance on development. *Id.* While the bank spent two years attempting to obtain zoning approval until it became clear zoning approval was not possible, the developer chose to continue with the property before zoning approval was granted, and there could be no claim for detrimental reliance. *Id.* at 22. Therefore, the court held that any assertion made by the property developer that it could have financially benefitted from the sale of the property was too speculative to serve as a basis for definite detriment. *Id.* at 24.

However, if a clear calculation of damages can be made, as to lost salary and additional costs suffered, it supports a claim of definite detrimental reliance. *Goldfarb v. Solimine*, 245 A.3d 570 (N.J. 2023); *Swider v. Ha-Lo Indus.*, 134 F. Supp. 2d 607, 620 (D.N.J. 2001) (holding that a calculation of lost salary is not enough to establish detrimental reliance; there must also be a calculation of additional costs spent in reliance on the promise). In *Goldfarb*, a financial analyst was promised employment by a prospective client in managing his financial portfolios. 245 A.3d at 572. In reliance on the promise, the analyst subsequently quit his job, where he was making between $308,000 and $466,000 per year. *Id.* at 573. The client then reneged on the offer and the analyst subsequently brought a claim for promissory estoppel. *Id.* The analyst was able to calculate a definite loss in salary based off his salary from the prior several years, the salary he was promised by the client, and the substantially lessened salary he received once he found a new job. *Id.* at 579. The court held that since the analyst could make a definite damage calculation by pointing to specific financial losses incurred in his reliance on the client's promise, there was a definite detriment, and a promissory estoppel claim could survive. *Id.* at 581.

Additionally, courts have not recognized any arguments for "roads not taken," or the search for other opportunities forgone, to establish substantial detriment, as such decisions are made by the promisee and not the promisor. *Malaker*, 395 A.2d at 232; *Friedman v. Tappan Dev. Corp.*, 126 A.2d 646, 652 (N.J. 1956) (holding that where a buyer of land backed out of a deal, the seller experienced no detriment because they could still sell the land to another). In *Malaker*, a corporation's stockholder committee brought suit against a bank under promissory estoppel for failing to follow through with an oral promise to lend the corporation money. 395 A.23d at 224. The stockholder committee asserted that in reliance on the bank's promise, it did not search for funding elsewhere, where it otherwise could have. *Id.* at 232. The court held that such an assertion is inherently speculative as the committee failed to furnish proof that it would have been granted loans elsewhere. *Id.* Thus, the court held that the failure to seek outside opportunities is not substantial enough to show detrimental reliance. *Id.*

Moreover, if the plaintiff has received most or all of the benefit from the promise, they may not subsequently make a claim of detrimental reliance and promissory estoppel. *Sadej v. Arturi*, 2019 N.J. Super. Unpub. LEXIS 1043 at *22 (Super. Ct. App. Div. 2019); *King James Care Ctr. Of Chatham 415 S. Blvd. Chatham v. Richardson*, 2018 N.J. Super. Unpub. LEXIS 4394 at *25–26 (holding where the promisee does not receive most or all of the benefit, there is a detriment). In *Sadej*, plaintiff homeowners filed and received approval for five pages of proposed improvements to their property and home. 2019 N.J. Super. Unpub. LEXIS at *1. After giving approval, the city subsequently rescinded their approval and issued a stop work order after the homeowners had constructed 80 percent of the improvements. *Id.* at 2. The homeowners were able to complete most of their projects, with the exception of attaching their detached garage. *Id.* at *23. Thus, the court held that since most of the projects were still completed with minimal delay, there was no substantial detriment that supported a claim for promissory estoppel. *Id.*

Mr. Li's claim for damages is purely speculative, and thus he cannot establish he suffered a definite detriment in order to support a claim of promissory estoppel against Micheo & Yoon. FACTS. Similarly in *Village Square*, the property development company could not definitively establish the financial gain, or lack thereof, that it could have received if the bank followed through with its promise. 2016 N.J. Super. Unpub. LEXIS 269 at *24. Furthermore, Mr. Li did not apply to any other big law firm positions, so any assertion that he could have gotten a job of a similar status and salary as Micheo & Yoon is purely speculative and cannot be proven. Thus Mr. Li cannot establish definite detriment to support a claim of promissory estoppel.

While the court has held that a clear calculation of damages may establish detriment and support a claim for promissory estoppel, Mr. Li cannot make a clear calculation of damages. Since Mr. Li was never actually offered a specific salary from Micheo &Yoon, there is no way to reasonably and specifically calculate damages relating to lost salary. This case can be distinguished from the case in *Goldfarb* where an analyst could use past earnings to establish a definite loss. 2019 N.J. Super. LEXIS at *1. In contrast, Mr. Li did not have prior full-time employment, nor was he promised a specific post-graduation salary. Thus Mr. Li did not give up a definite salary and therefore cannot establish a definite detriment in reliance on the promise.

Similarly, there was no substantial detriment as Mr. Li was not prevented from seeking outside opportunities in the first place. While Ms. Heinan's offer was attractive, there was no communication, either made by Ms. Heinan in the offer or from any other representative of Micheo & Yoon, that attempted to discourage Mr. Li from searching elsewhere for employment. The courts have held that discussion over "roads not taken" is likewise too speculative to be used to establish substantial detriment. *Malaker*, 395 A.2d at 232. Just as in *Malaker*, where a stockholder committee did not search for outside loan funding, *id.*, Mr. Li actively chose not to interview with any other law firm. Such a decision was made completely by Mr. Li, without outside influence or control. Even though Mr. Li exhibited attractive career qualities early on, based on his decision to decline outside interviews, he cannot establish substantial detriment and therefore cannot support a claim for promissory estoppel.

Finally, Mr. Li has not been without benefit in relying on Micheo & Yoon's promise as he gained the benefit of working for a "big law" firm. Mr. Li was able to get two summers of experience at a prestigious law firm, while also saving money by working in his home state. Such experience has operated to strengthen his marketability and bolster his resume in an unstable job market. The *Sadej* court held that a promisee who received all or most of the benefit cannot establish the detriment element of promissory estoppel. 2019 N.J. Super. Unpub. LEXIS at *1. Just as in *Sadej*, *id.*, where the plaintiff homeowners benefitted by being able to make 80 percent of their planned improvements, Mr. Li was benefitted by gaining two summers of experience. Since Mr. Li received a benefit from working at Micheo & Yoon during law school, a benefit that now resides on his resume and enhances his marketability, he cannot at the same time establish a detriment in support of promissory estoppel.

Mr. Li did not experience a detriment in his reliance on Micheo & Yoon's conditional offer. Mr. Li cannot establish a definite detriment because his claim is purely speculative as he cannot provide opportunity or economic baseline. He actively chose to not explore other employment opportunities, he had no prior salary baseline, and Micheo & Yoon did not promise a specific starting salary. Likewise, he is unable to establish a substantial detriment as Micheo & Yoon did not encourage the forbearance of other employment opportunities, and either way, the courts do not allow a "roads not taken" argument. Furthermore, Mr. Li received a tangible benefit from his summers with Micheo & Yoon, thus bolstering his employability in an unstable job market.

CONCLUSION

Mr. Li cannot support a claim for promissory estoppel because he cannot establish the elements of reasonable reliance and detrimental reliance. Mr. Li was not reasonable in relying on Micheo & Yoon's conditional offer due to his failure to satisfy the conditions of the promise, the temporal gap between the time the promise was made and its expected date of maturation, and external economic forces beyond the firm's control.

Similarly, Mr. Li cannot establish that he experienced a detriment because he cannot point to anything definite or substantial. He is unable to establish a definite detriment because his claims are speculative, and his alleged damages are unable to be clearly and unambiguously calculated. He is also unable to establish a substantial detriment as it was his own conduct and decisions that prevented him from finding other employment. Additionally, he received a tangible benefit from his summer employment he completed in reliance on the promise.

WHEREFORE, Defendant, MICHEO & YOON, respectfully requests that this Honorable Court grant this Motion for Summary Judgment as to Plaintiff's Complaint and order any further relief as this Court deems appropriate.

CERTIFICATE OF SERVICE

I HEREBY CERTIFY, that on this _____ day of _________ 2024, a true and correct copy of the foregoing has been filed with the Clerk of Courts via Electronic Case Filing with a copy to be served on Opposing Counsel of Lawyer, Attorney & Esquire, P.A., 123 Address Road, City, State Zip, ocounsel@lawyerattorneyesquire.com.

LAW FIRM, P.A.
s/ Nora Maloney
NORA MALONEY, ESQ.
Bar No.:1234567
456 Location Drive
City, State Zip
Telephone: (123) 456-7890
Service Email:
nmaloney@lawfirm.com
Attorney for Defendant

NINETEEN

Tips for Oral Argument

For many law students, oral argument is the most exhilarating, yet anxiety-producing, part of the first-year legal writing program. This chapter briefly addresses how to transfer the strong analysis of your writing into an equally strong oral argument. It will focus on appellate argument, but you can easily adapt these tips to oral arguments for motions.

A well-written brief can go a long way in supporting your oral argument. In legal practice, the success of the case typically rides on the brief. Only a small percentage of briefs are actually selected for oral argument; most judges decide the case based solely on the briefs. Judges hear oral arguments only when they want clarification on issues within the brief.

Although you will use your brief to outline your oral argument, your oral argument is not simply a replication of your brief. In a 1L or moot court competition, your judges will not likely have read your brief before hearing your argument, so you should not feel wed to its content when you argue. Moreover, you will not have the time to simply read your brief. You must outline your most important legal points as they apply to the facts of your case.

Appellate oral arguments lack much of the drama of trial arguments. In an oral argument, the attorneys do not address a jury, or even each other. There are no witnesses to call. Instead the advocates are arguing the merits of the case before a judge or panel of judges. The appellant will argue first and will be able to reserve time for a rebuttal. The appellee will argue next, and the appellant will then present a short rebuttal.

What tends to be most nerve wracking for students is that the judges can interrupt oral argument repeatedly with any questions they may have for the advocate. A strong oral advocate will organize her oral argument similar to the way she organizes the analysis. All oral arguments begin with "May it please the court," followed by an impact statement that incorporates the theory of the case and a very brief roadmap of what is at issue. The roadmap should be signposted, meaning that if there are two issues before the court, the advocate will identify the issue through a prayer.

For example, "This Court should grant summary judgment on behalf of the appellant for two reasons: first…" followed by the legal conclusion on the first issue, and "second…" followed by the legal conclusion on the second issue. These conclusions are simply conclusions; they do not include a factual basis as may your brief's point headings.

The advocate can then segue into the first issue by saying something to the effect of "turning to the first issue" and then beginning with an assertion. Just like the argument in the written brief, the oral argument will be organized by assertion. If it works logically, the advocate should put the most important assertions first in case the advocate runs out of time to finish. Each assertion will be followed by relevant facts of the case, and, just as in the brief, where appropriate the advocate will make comparisons to cases that were decided on that issue in a way that would be favorable if applied to her client.

The table below illustrates the general structure of the appellant's and appellee's respective oral arguments.

TABLE 1.

Appellant (or Petitioner)	Appellee (or Respondent)
Introduction (name and "may it please the court")	Introduction (name and "may it please the court")
Theory of the Case: In a sentence or two, tell the judges what the case is about.	Theory of the Case: In a sentence or two, tell the judges what the case is about.
This court should reverse ... (i.e., state your prayer) for [number] reasons (frame as short legal conclusions)	This court should affirm its holding that ... (i.e., state your prayer) for [number] reasons (frame as short legal conclusions)
Ask "your honors" whether they would like to hear a brief recitation of the facts. Only the appellant needs to be prepared with the facts.	
Turn to your first argument and continue.	Turn to your first argument and continue.
If time permits, briefly conclude.	If time permits, briefly conclude.
A rebuttal: Your rebuttal should bring home one or two points at most. You should not use it to complete your legal argument. Instead, focus on "bringing home" a major point or reinforcing a weakness that a judge pointed out during argument. Even better, if you can, incorporate the judge's name. For example, "as Judge Smith noted...."	Although the appellee does not have a formal rebuttal, it can incorporate the equivalent in the argument. It is impressive when the appellee is responsive in argument to a couple of major questions or statements by judges during the appellant's argument.

PROF'S TIPS

You have stated the number of reasons the court should find in your client's favor. Accordingly, as you get to each argument, signpost them by numbering each argument (i.e. use words like "first" and "second." This will help the listener to follow the organization of your argument.

Remember:

- You are not merely reading your brief. Think of yourself as teaching the judges the law as it applies to the facts of your case.
- This is a conversation that can change direction anytime the judges ask a question. If they take you to a different assertion, answer the question, continue to address that assertion, and if there is time, circle back to complete an incomplete or unaddressed issue.
- Do not use "I." Moreover, do not say "I think," "I would say," "I believe," etc. It is best to simply state your assertion even when answering a question. If you must insert yourself, you can use the royal "we" as in "we contend," or you can state your position in third-party terms of "the appellant would argue" or "the appellee contends."
- Address the judge as "your honor," not "sir' or "ma'am." Your tone should be conversational but not colloquial. Remain deferential. When a judge asks a question, immediately stop speaking and pay attention. You must never interrupt a judge.
- Sometimes a judge will interrupt your answer even as you are responding to a question. Immediately answer and then try to return to responding to the initial question.

PROF'S TIPS

If the Chief Judge or Justice has asked one of the questions, answer that question first.

- If you are confronted with a compound question from one or more judges, signpost your answer by saying something to the effect that you will address Judge Smith's question first and then you will answer Judge Jackson's. If you forget part of the question, it is fine to ask the judge to repeat the question.
- Again, it is fine to ask a judge to repeat a question, or to admit that you are unfamiliar with the facts of a particular case.
- In using cases to support your argument, include the full case name the first time you say it (i.e., "Acme versus Ace"). Use "versus" and not "v." Also, identify the court. "In Acme versus Ace, this Court held…" or "in Acme versus Ace, the Supreme Court held…." After providing the full name of a case, you can default to using the first name. Refer to statutes by short name.

- In your note sheets, you should also have a brief outline of the major points in your argument. You should also have the cases that support those arguments. Include the case name, year, and court for the major cases, and include brief descriptions of the case where you need them. In some instances, you may want to include some record cites to support important facts.
- Memorize your introduction.
- Be prepared to compare favorable cases and distinguish unfavorable ones.
- Do not bring several pages of materials. You do not want to flip pages or note cards at the podium.
- Keep gestures to a minimum. While you do not have to be stiff, you do not want your movements to distract the judges from your argument. If it helps, hold onto the podium to limit gesturing.
- Your eye contact should be with the judges and no one else in the room.
- Be respectful and deferential to your judges. Do not argue with them!
- Both sides should understand the standard of review.
- Since 1L brief problems are often based on appeal from summary judgment, appellants should highlight any judicial questions or comments that raise the possibility that there is a genuine issue of material fact that warrants the case going trial. To the contrary, appellees should not make an argument that raises that likelihood.
- Slow down. Take the time to think about and answer judges' questions. Do not go into oral argument with the objective of simply getting through your arguments. Instead, your objective should be to leave the judges with a thorough understanding of why the law and policies are in favor of your client.
- If you have thoroughly addressed your important arguments, it is okay to end your presentation before your time is up.
- If you are out of time, finish your sentence and say, "Thank you." You may say to a judge, "May I briefly conclude?" and then proceed to finish in fewer than twenty seconds. If you are in the middle of answering a judge's question as you run out of time, say to the

judge, "Your honor, I see I have run out of time; may I finish answering your question?" If the judge answers in the affirmative, briefly finish your answer, say thank you, and return to your seat. Do not try to conclude after answering the question.

- Questions are not inherently antagonistic. When feasible, look at questions as opportunities rather than challenges.
- Do not thank a judge for a question or tell a judge that the question was a good one; it sounds condescending.
- Sometimes you must concede a point. When you do, have at the ready an alternative reason your client should win.
- As you practice your oral argument, practice transitioning among points after answering questions. If a judge asks a question that takes you from one assertion to another, answer the judge's question thoroughly and continue to make the argument relevant to that question. If you have time, circle back to earlier points.
- You likely know more about the case and its legal issues than the judge. Be confident in that knowledge. Although you have an agenda, stay in control while remaining deferential to what is most important or interesting to the judges.
- Be responsive to the question the judge is asking. This includes beginning a response to a "yes-no" question with a "yes" or a "no" followed by your explanation.
- If you do not know the answer to a question, you should admit it.
- It is okay to pause and think about the answer to a question before answering it.
- Practice, practice, and practice some more. Ideally, you should practice with others who will interrupt you and ask questions. Practice with questions in different forms and different sequences. The goal is to sound comfortable and conversational, rather than rehearsed and canned.

END OF CHAPTER SUMMARY

- Incorporate the theory of your case.
- Follow the formal structure of the oral argument.
- Signpost your argument.
- Organize by assertion just as you would in your analysis.
- Incorporate case law to support your legal points.
- Listen carefully to the judge's questions and answer them.
- Show appropriate deference.

PART III

Writing beyond the Classroom

TWENTY

From Writing Class to Writing Sample

This chapter provides guidance with respect to editing your memorandum or brief into a suitable writing sample.

TWENTY-ONE

Using Your Skills to Write a Persuasive Cover Letter

This chapter takes the skills you developed in writing a persuasive legal document and transfers them to pitching yourself to a potential legal employer.

TWENTY-TWO

From Class Memorandum to e-Memorandum

This chapter demonstrates how to condense a formal memorandum to the e-memorandum legal employers often request.

TWENTY

From Writing Class to Writing Sample

It is likely that you will need to use your graded memorandum or brief as the writing sample in pursuit of a legal job. Often you will have to adapt the legal document you wrote in class to conform with the requirements of the prospective employer. The first alteration you should make is an ethical one; you need to include a statement that although your writing sample is your original work product, it also incorporates feedback from your writing professor. You can create a cover sheet or a preface to the writing sample itself.

Your next consideration should be the length of the document. Some legal organizations do not include a page limit, but most have a page limit of five or ten pages. If your writing sample exceeds the page limit, you should eliminate sections to meet the requirements while still giving your prospective employer a sense of your abilities. If you have to reduce the length of your writing sample, be sure to include in your preface or cover page explaining that you edited the document to meet length requirements, but that you can provide the entire document upon request.

Order of Elimination

The first section you should eliminate is the Statement of Facts; you can keep the heading, eliminate the prose underneath, and replace the prose with "omitted to meet page length requirements" or similar language. Your prospective employers are unlikely to read a Statement of Facts; if your analysis is thorough, they will easily be able to glean the legal context and legally relevant facts.

If your document is still too long, eliminate other sections, but keep the Discussion (if it is a memorandum) or Argument (if it is a brief or other persuasive document) content. This is the section that truly reflects your ability to organize your research to analyze a legal issue and is therefore what an employer most wants to review. If your discussion—or argument—section is still too long, select a subsection that includes an entire CREACC. Select the subsection on which you received the most positive comments from the professor who graded your work. If that is unclear, think about your reader. Which CREACC is easiest to follow? Which CREACC best reflects your ability to take a sophisticated legal concept and deftly break it down for a reader who is unfamiliar with the fact pattern and law. If the document is a persuasive one, select the CREACC that reflects your strongest argument. Or if you had to balance factors, select an argument where you did that effectively.

This is your opportunity to showcase your writing abilities, so select what will really make you shine. Even if your professor provided you with extensive feedback, take the time to carefully proofread and edit your work even after incorporating feedback.

END OF CHAPTER SUMMARY

- Shorten your writing so that it is from five to ten pages total.
- Include the portion that highlights your analysis.
- Check for typographical and citation errors.

TWENTY-ONE

Using Your Skills to Write a Persuasive Cover Letter

What you learn about organization and analysis in your legal writing class should serve you thereafter—whether it be on your exams, writing for law school extracurricular activities (e.g., journal, moot court, mock trial, etc.), summer legal work, or your legal career. You should even be able to incorporate what you learned when you are writing your cover letters. You may wonder how writing a cover letter relates to legal writing, but a cover letter is a persuasive document in which you are marketing yourself. Think about what would appeal to a reader looking to hire a law student for the summer. You want a student with demonstrated academic and work ethic, but you primarily want a student who can research, write, and analyze. Your cover letter should highlight your strengths and include specific examples of activities in which you have engaged that could bring value to the legal organization.

I am often surprised by how poorly students market themselves. Every student who gets into law school should be able to highlight the skills that would appeal to a prospective employer. Often students will follow their brief introduction with a statement about the prominence of the legal organization. News flash: the organization already knows of its own prominence; you need to talk about what *you* will bring to it. The information that follows provides a general outline of the content of a strong cover letter. You do not have to follow it precisely; adapt it so that it works for you.

The First Paragraph Is Your Introductory Paragraph

This is the paragraph in which you introduce yourself and include your year and the name of your law school. If you have any connection to the legal organization or a special passion for the work it does, this is the place to include it. You should also include language to the effect that you are confident that your skills and abilities would make you an asset to the organization; if you can categorize those skills and abilities, even better.

The Second Paragraph Typically Begins with What You Have Accomplished in Law School

Unless there is something in your background that warrants particular highlighting, the cover letter should generally be structured reverse chronologically. Accordingly, the second paragraph should discuss your current performance and accomplishments at law school. Highlight your class rank if it is high and any strengths in your coursework, particularly courses that are relevant to the job. For example, if you are interested in litigation and you performed particularly well in Civil Procedure, point that out; likewise, if you are interested in transactional work and earned a high grade in Contracts, note it. If you have a reason why you are interested in a specific practice area, this is where you explain that. Every potential employer wants to know that you can write well, so if you performed particularly well in your legal writing class or on your final writing project, please note that. This is where you point out leadership and relevant extracurricular work. If you have little to write about law school accomplishments, create a transition into work experience and focus primarily on that.

The Third—and Possibly Fourth—Paragraph Is About What You Did Prior to Enrolling at Your Law School

The remainder of the cover letter should focus on academic and professional accomplishments. For example, if you graduated with Latin honors from your undergraduate institution write: I am a *summa cum laude* graduate of x institution. The bonus is that the italics for Latin honors stand out. If you are transitioning from a previous career, this is the place to explain why you are making the transition (i.e., what inspired you to pursue a legal career) and how the skills you acquired prior to entering law school will bring value to the field you are pursuing.

Although your cover letter should not replicate your resume completely, take the time to expand on any experience that highlights your writing and/or analytical prowess. Honors theses, publications, and debate awards are just a few. Leadership and other recognitions are also important. If you worked through college or had a double major, include that information. This is not the time to be modest. Along with your G.P.A. and LSAT scores, there are multiple reasons your law school's admission team admitted you; give your prospective employers equally compelling reasons to hire you.

PROF'S TIPS

Note that this is a typical 1L letter in which the writer has not had much legal work experience. The emphasis in a 2L letter will include information on experience from the 1L summer.

A FEW MORE TIPS

- Avoid putting your emotions in your cover letter unless you are applying to a job in the public service. Writing that you are really excited about the prospect of working at an entity is pretty meaningless in and of itself, but if you have a passion for a particular field in the public interest arena (e.g., environmental justice), it is appropriate to include in your introduction.
- Do not write that you are interested in a job because it is family friendly or offers a work-life balance, even if the job includes information like that on its website. Many employers will see that statement from you as one in which you are more interested in time off than work.
- Instead of writing that you have a strong work ethic, leadership qualities, or a similar descriptor, include experience that will lead the reader to that conclusion. This experience does not have to be legal or law-related experience (e.g., juggling a part-time job while maintaining a high G.P.A. in an honors program).
- If you had to try out for any of the extracurriculars you list, note that you were *competitively selected* for the position.
- I said it before, and I will say it again: highlight activities that require research, writing, and analysis. This does not have to be law related. If you have a math or science background that requires data analysis, include it.
- Read your letter aloud and then have at least two other people you trust to review your finished product. Typographical errors can cost you a job offer!

Sample Cover Letters

Your address

Month, date, year
Mr. John Doe
Legal Recruiting and Development Coordinator
Firm
Address

Dear Mr. Doe:

I am a first-year law student at Law University, and I am seeking a Summer Associate position with Law Firm. I met Angela Roe at a networking event at Law University, and she encouraged me to submit my materials to you. I am confident that my previous legal experience, my strong writing and analytical skills, and my interest in litigation would make me an asset to your summer program.

> **PROF'S TIPS**
> You should always highlight the general strengths that would bring value to the organization. Writing and analysis are two such assets.

At Law University, I am on the Dean's List; I earned an A in Civil Procedure and an A+ on my final memorandum in my Legal Writing and Analysis course. I have balanced a challenging course load with active membership in the South Asian Law Students' Association and Law University's Corporate Law Society. Prior to enrolling in Law University, I interned for Southern Public Interest Organization where I drafted memoranda summarizing the status of multiple homelessness and gender change measures in city commissions throughout Florida. I further developed the organizational and writing skills I gained in this position at the Law Offices of Richard Roe where I collected and preserved documents of wrongdoing against our clients in preparation for trial. I also worked directly with potential clients to create reports that senior counsel would use to determine whether to adopt a new client. I credit these early legal experiences with my success in my first-semester legal writing course where I earned one of only two As in my legal writing section.

> **PROF'S TIPS**
> Usually you will begin your second paragraph with your accomplishments at your law school. Begin with academic highlights followed by extracurricular activities and leadership.

> **PROF'S TIPS**
> When you include work experience, highlight activities that require writing, analysis, research, and initiative. Do not state your qualities; use your experience to tell the story.

PROF'S TIPS
If you earned Latin honors you should include and italicize them. Latin terms are generally italicized, so that emphasis will draw your reader's attention to the honorific.

I graduated *cum laude* from Undergraduate University with a dual degree in political science and economics; my coursework primarily focused on the influence of regulatory and legislative changes on consumer behavior. While I pursued my bachelor's degree, I also participated in mock trial; I would love to continue developing my skills in litigation and the law within Law Firm's litigation or government relations team.

PROF'S TIPS
Include extracurricular and leadership experience.

Thank you for your time and consideration of my application materials. If you have any questions about my qualifications or application, please do not hesitate to contact me at (321) 555-0525 or at suresh.boodram@lawschool.edu.

Sincerely,
[insert handwritten/or script font signature]
Suresh Boodram

Your address

Month day, year
Jane Doe
Chief of Staff
Public Service Organization
Alphabet Street NE
Washington, DC 20054

PROF'S TIPS
If you are passionate about a particular aspect of a public interest job, you should let the reader know.

Dear Ms. Doe:

I am a first-year law student at Law University and writing to express my interest in an internship position within Public Service Organization for the Summer year term. I have a demonstrated interest in economic impact on government policy, and I have always been passionate about the impact of those policies on the poor. I am confident that my professional interests and my academic strengths—particularly in writing and legal analysis—would make me an asset to your organization.

At Law University, I was especially interested in Contract doctrine, and I earned an A in that class. I was also able to build upon my analytical strengths in my legal writing class in which I was one of only two students in the class to earn an A. I also am a first-year representative for Law University's Public Interest Society and a member of the South Asian Law Students' Association.

Prior to enrolling at Law University, I graduated *magna cum laude* from Undergraduate University where I majored in economics and minored in English literature while working a part-time job the last two years of college. During my senior year at Undergraduate University, I wrote an honors thesis that focused on the market factors that influence competition and the harmful effects of monopolistic conduct.

PROF'S TIPS

If you do not have many extracurriculars because you worked through school, be sure to let your reader know that you worked.

PROF'S TIPS

If you wrote an honors thesis or completed an important academic project, highlight it.

While I pursued my degrees in economics and political science, I interned for Southern Public Interest Organization where I drafted memoranda summarizing the status of multiple homelessness and transgender measures in city commissions throughout Florida. After I graduated from Undergraduate University, I further developed my writing skills at the Law Offices of John Doe where I collected and preserved documents of wrongdoing against our clients in preparation for trial; I also created reports that senior counsel would use to determine whether to adopt a new client. These experienced inspired me to pursue a legal career in which I could advocate on behalf of those who lack access to many legal resources.

Thank you for your time and consideration. If you have any questions about my qualifications or application, please do not hesitate to contact me at (321) 555-0525 or at suresh.boodram@lawschool.edu.

Sincerely,
[insert handwritten/or script font signature]
Suresh Boodram

END OF CHAPTER SUMMARY

- Organize your cover letter according to traditional structure.
- Think about your audience and highlight those experiences, achievements, and interests that are consistent with what your employer is seeking. This includes, but is not limited to: academic honors awards; experiences that require research, writing, and analysis; leadership experience; and fundraising; handling significant multi-tasks (e.g., working through college).
- Do not write everything on your resume, but do not be afraid to repeat important information from your resume.
- Check for typographical errors.

TWENTY-TWO

From Class Memorandum to e-Memorandum

I tell my students that during their summers, they are probably more likely to be asked to write an email memorandum than a formal memorandum. We legal writing professors teach you to write the formal memorandum because it provides the structure necessary to write a legal document. It is easier to simplify a formal memorandum than it is to learn the abbreviated version and then not be able to write the unabridged version, should your supervisor request that.

If your supervisor asks you to provide a legal answer in an informal email, you will need to make some adaptations. That supervisor will not want the length or formality of a longer memorandum. Instead, you need to be able to include your analysis in a readable email format that should not require the reader to scroll. Typically, your supervisor will provide some guidance with respect to the parameters, but below are a few general guidelines:

- Include the memorandum topic in the email subject line.
- Do not include the addressee's email address until you complete and proofread your memorandum; you do not want to inadvertently send your email before you complete it.
- You do not need to include a Statement of Facts, formal Question(s) Presented, Brief Answer(s), Conclusion, or even a formal Discussion section.

- Instead of writing a CREACC, you will write your answer more in the style of a law school exam's Issue, Rule, Analysis and Counter-Analysis, Conclusion format. Begin with a statement that identifies the subject you were asked to research; include and cite any applicable rules of law; analyze the rule of law by applying it to your situation. Include applicable law for your situation; include both analysis and counter-analysis as applicable. Include a one-sentence conclusion for the issue.
- The total length of this email should be fairly short—the equivalent of no more than a single page. Some supervisors even ask you organize by bullets.
- Even though the structure of the email memorandum may be abbreviated, your language should be as formal as that of an unabridged one.

Sample e-Memorandum

Prose Version

From: Boodram, Suresh <suresh.boodram@lawschool.edu>
Sent: Monday, August 9, 2024 1:14 PM
To: Pinder, Kamina A. <kamina.aliya.pinder@lawschool.edu>
Subject: Sample (Prose Edition)—Memorandum on Spencer Li's Promissory Estoppel Claim

Dear X,

You asked me to research whether Mr. Li can support a claim of promissory estoppel against Micheo & Yoon. Specifically, you asked whether Mr. Li could establish that his reliance on the law firm's promise of post-graduation employment made the summer after Mr. Li's first year employment was reasonable, and that this reliance resulted in definite and substantial detriment to Mr. Li. Under New Jersey law, Mr. Li will have difficulty establishing a prima facie claim of promissory estoppel because he did not reasonably rely on Micheo & Yoon's promise to employ him after he graduated because the promise was made too remote in time from when it could be fulfilled, it is possible Mr. Li did not meet the conditions of the promise, and external economic pressures affected the law firm's ability to fulfill its promise to Mr. Li. Likewise, Mr. Li cannot establish the essential factors of a definite and substantial detriment because Mr. Li's lost potential earnings are mere speculation and it was his choice to forgo other employment prospects. I have included my analysis of these issues below.

Issue One: Whether Mr. Li Can Establish Reasonable Reliance?

Mr. Li likely cannot support a claim of promissory estoppel because it was not reasonable for Mr. Li to rely on Micheo & Yoon's promise of future employment if he did not meet the law firm's conditions to Mr. Li's post-graduation employment.

To satisfy the third element of a claim for promissory estoppel, a plaintiff must show that he reasonably relied on a representation made by the defendant, which induced him to abandon an existing right or influenced him to act or refrain from acting. *Friedman v. Tappan Dev. Corp.*, 126 A.2d 646, 653 (N.J. 1956). When the promisee does not satisfy the conditions of the promise, the court is unlikely to hold that reliance on the promise is reasonable. *Bonczek v. Carter-Wallace, Inc.*, 701 A.2d 742, 744–46 (N.J. Super. Ct. App. Div. 1997). Ms. Heinan specifically told Mr. Li that he had to keep up a "high G.P.A." in order to receive an offer in his last year of law school. Though Mr. Li had a G.P.A. of 3.8 when Ms. Heinan made the promise, Mr. Li purposefully "relaxed" his work ethic and allowed his G.P.A. to drop to a 3.5. Mr. Li could claim that he met the conditions of the agreement because he was still on the Dean's List and on journal. However, because Mr. Li let his grades drop and the condition of a high G.P.A. would likely be defined by the law firm's prior policy, a court likely would not consider Mr. Li's reliance reasonable.

It was also not reasonable for Mr. Li to rely on Micheo & Yoon's promise of employment because the promise was made too distant in time from its expected fulfillment. New Jersey courts have held that an employee who relied on an employer's promise made two years in the past did not reasonably rely on the promise because the promise was too far removed from the date of maturation. *Thomas v. Princeton Univ.*, No. A-0680-14T1, 2016 N.J. Super. Unpub. LEXIS 2515, at *10 (Super. Ct. App. Div. Nov. 23, 2016). Ms. Heinan made the promise to employ Mr. Li almost two years before Mr. Li would be able to take the position. Additionally, Ms. Heinan only mentioned extending such an offer at a distant point in the future.

The external economic forces that affected the law firm's ability to deliver on its promise were likely such that it was unreasonable for Mr. Li to rely on the promise of employment. New Jersey courts have held that when there are viable business reasons for not hiring someone and budgetary cutbacks, it is not reasonable to rely on a promise of employment. *E. Orange Bd. of Educ. v. N.J. Sch. Const. Corp.*, 963 A.2d 865, 874–75 (N.J. Super. Ct. App. Div. 2009). When Ms. Heinan informed Mr. Li that the firm could no longer employ him, many firms were also experiencing a decrease in job availability due to the moderate economic recession. In the context of a slowing economy, which was evident at the time Ms. Heinan made the promise to Mr. Li, it would likely not be reasonable to rely on such a promise. Because Mr. Li may not have met the conditions of the promise, was offered employment two years before he could take the position, and there were negative economic factors beyond the law firm's control impacting its ability to hire Mr. Li, the court will likely hold that it was not reasonable for Mr. Li to rely on Ms. Heinan's promise of employment.

Issue Two: Whether Mr. Li's Reliance Resulted in Definite and Substantial Detriment to Mr. Li?

Mr. Li likely cannot establish that he suffered a definite detriment as a result of Micheo & Yoon's promise because his alleged damages are speculative as there is no way to calculate the exact damages Mr. Li incurred.

In New Jersey, there are two essential components that must be present to establish the element of detrimental reliance: (1) a definite detriment and (2) a substantial detriment. *Malaker Corp. Stockholders Protective Comm. v. First Jersey Nat'l Bank*, 163 N.J. Super. 463 (Super. Ct. App. Div. 1978). Where a plaintiff cannot establish that he or she could have achieved financial gain by exercising alternative options, the plaintiff cannot support detriment. *Village Square Madison Ave., LLC v. TD Bank, N.A.*, 2016 N.J. Super. LEXIS 269 at *24. Mr. Li did not apply to any other law firm positions, so there is no way to prove he could have acquired a legal job of the same caliber and salary as Micheo & Yoon. Mr. Li could try to establish a definite method to calculate his lost earnings by comparing the salary he would have made with Micheo & Yoon to his current salary. When there is a clear way to prove economic loss, the court may find there is a definite detriment. *Goldfarb v. Solimine*, No. A-3740-

16T2, 2019 N.J. Super. LEXIS 1472, at *1, 28 (Super. Ct. App. Div. June 26, 2019). However, Mr. Li had no past earnings and did not forgo current employment, so he did not give up a definite salary to work with Micheo & Yoon.

Just as there is no definite detriment, Mr. Li also did not suffer a substantial detriment because Mr. Li was not prevented from seeking opportunities with other law firms. Using forgone potential opportunities as the way to establish detrimental reliance is too speculative to establish a substantial detriment. *Malaker*, 395 A.2d at 232. While Mr. Li was told he would receive an offer if he continued to work with Micheo & Yoon, the law firm never dissuaded Mr. Li from applying to other firms. When Mr. Li failed to seek alternative employment, he precluded any opportunity to determine whether he would have received another job offer from a top law firm, and how much he would have made there. Mr. Li cannot likely establish that Micheo & Yoon's broken promise of future employment incurred definite or substantial detriment because Mr. Li did not lose any assured income, it would be too speculative to calculate potential lost earnings, and Micheo & Yoon did not prevent Mr. Li from seeking alternative employment opportunities at any time.

Bulleted Version

From: Boodram, Suresh <suresh.boodram@lawschool.edu>
Sent: Monday, August 9, 2024 1:14 PM
To: Pinder, Kamina A. <kamina.aliya.pinder@lawschool.edu>
Subject: Sample (Bullet Point Edition)—Memorandum on Spencer Li's Promissory Estoppel Claim

Hello,

You asked me to research whether Mr. Li can support a claim of promissory estoppel against Micheo & Yoon. Specifically, you asked whether Mr. Li could establish that his reliance on the law firm's promise of post-graduation employment made the summer after Mr. Li's first year employment was reasonable, and that this reliance resulted in definite and substantial detriment to Mr. Li.

Under New Jersey law, Mr. Li will have difficulty establishing a prima facie claim of promissory estoppel because he did not reasonably rely on Micheo & Yoon's promise to employ him after he graduated because the promise was made too remote in time from when it could be fulfilled, it is possible Mr. Li did not meet the conditions of the promise, and external economic pressures affected the law firm's ability to fulfill its promise to Mr. Li. Likewise, Mr. Li cannot establish the essential factors of a definite and substantial detriment because Mr. Li's lost potential earnings are mere speculation and it was his choice to forgo other employment prospects. My analysis of the respective issues is below.

- **Issue One: Whether Mr. Li Can Establish Reasonable Reliance?**

  Because Mr. Li may not have met the conditions of the promise, was offered employment two years before he could take the position, and there were negative economic factors beyond the law firm's control impacting its ability to hire Mr. Li, the court will likely hold that it was not reasonable for Mr. Li to rely on Ms. Heinan's promise of employment.

  Mr. Li likely cannot support a claim of promissory estoppel because it was not reasonable for Mr. Li to rely on Micheo & Yoon's promise of future employment if he did not meet the law firm's conditions to Mr. Li's post-graduation employment.

  - To satisfy the third element of a claim for promissory estoppel, a plaintiff must show that he reasonably relied on a representation made by the defendant, which induced him to abandon an existing right or influenced him to act or refrain from acting. *Friedman v. Tappan Dev. Corp.*, 126 A.2d 646, 653 (N.J. 1956).
    - When the promisee does not satisfy the conditions of the promise, the court is unlikely to hold that reliance on the promise is reasonable. *Bonczek v. Carter-Wallace, Inc.*, 701 A.2d 742, 744–46 (N.J. Super. Ct. App. Div. 1997).
    - Ms. Heinan specifically told Mr. Li that he had to keep up a "high G.P.A." in order to receive an offer in his last year of law school. Though Mr. Li had a G.P.A. of 3.8 when Ms. Heinan made the promise, Mr. Li purposefully "relaxed" his work ethic and allowed his G.P.A. to drop to a 3.5.
    - Mr. Li could claim that he met the conditions of the agreement because he was still on the Dean's List and on journal. However, because Mr. Li let his grades drop and the condition of a high G.P.A. would likely be defined by the law firm's prior policy, a court likely would not consider Mr. Li's reliance reasonable.

- It was also unreasonable for Mr. Li to rely on Micheo & Yoon's promise of employment because the promise was made too distant in time from its expected fulfillment.
    - New Jersey courts have held that an employee who relied on an employer's promise made two years in the past did not reasonably rely on the promise because the promise was too far removed from the date of maturation. *Thomas v. Princeton Univ.*, No. A-0680-14T1, 2016 N.J. Super. Unpub. LEXIS 2515, at *10 (Super. Ct. App. Div. Nov. 23, 2016).
    - Ms. Heinan made the promise to employ Mr. Li almost two years before Mr. Li would be able to take the position. Additionally, Ms. Heinan only mentioned extending such an offer at a distant point in the future.
- The external economic forces that affected the law firm's ability to deliver on its promise were likely such that it was unreasonable for Mr. Li to rely on the promise of employment.
    - New Jersey courts have held that when there are viable business reasons for not hiring someone and budgetary cutbacks, it is not reasonable to rely on a promise of employment. *E. Orange Bd. of Educ. v. N.J. Sch. Const. Corp.*, 963 A.2d 865, 874–75 (N.J. Super. Ct. App. Div. 2009).
    - When Ms. Heinan informed Mr. Li that the firm could no longer employ him, many firms were also experiencing a decrease in job availability due to the moderate economic recession. In the context of a slowing economy, which was evident at the time Ms. Heinan made the promise to Mr. Li, it would likely not be reasonable to rely on such a promise.

- **Issue Two: Whether Mr. Li's Reliance Resulted in Definite and Substantial Detriment to Mr. Li?**

Mr. Li cannot likely establish that Micheo & Yoon's broken promise of future employment incurred definite or substantial detriment because Mr. Li did not lose any assured income, it would be too speculative to calculate potential lost earnings, and Micheo & Yoon did not prevent Mr. Li from seeking alternative employment opportunities at any time.

Mr. Li likely cannot establish that he suffered a definite detriment as a result of Micheo & Yoon's promise because his alleged damages are speculative as there is no way to calculate the exact damages Mr. Li incurred.

- In New Jersey, there are two essential components that must be present to establish the element of detrimental reliance: (1) a definite detriment and (2) a substantial detriment. *Malaker Corp. Stockholders Protective Comm. v. First Jersey Nat'l Bank*, 163 N.J. Super. 463 (Super. Ct. App. Div. 1978).
  - Where the plaintiff could not establish that it could have achieved financial gain had it exercised alternative options, Mr. Li did not apply to any other law firm positions, so there is no way to prove he could have acquired a legal job of the same caliber and salary as Micheo & Yoon. *Village Square Madison Ave., LLC v. TD Bank, N.A.*, 2016 N.J. Super. LEXIS 269 at *24.
  - Mr. Li could try to establish a definite method to calculate his lost earnings by comparing the salary he would have made with Micheo & Yoon to his current salary. When there is a clear way to prove economic loss, the court may find there is a definite detriment. *Goldfarb v. Solimine*, No. A-3740-16T2, 2019 N.J. Super. LEXIS 1472, at *1, 28 (Super. Ct. App. Div. June 26, 2019). However, Mr. Li had no past earnings and did not forgo current employment, so he did not give up a definite salary to work with Micheo & Yoon.
- Just as there is no definite detriment, Mr. Li also did not suffer a substantial detriment because Mr. Li was not prevented from seeking opportunities with other law firms.
  - Using forgone potential opportunities as the way to establish detrimental reliance is too speculative to establish a substantial detriment. *Malaker*, 395 A.2d at 232.
  - While Mr. Li was told he would receive an offer if he continued to work with Micheo & Yoon, the law firm never dissuaded Mr. Li from applying to other firms. When Mr. Li failed to seek alternative employment, he precluded any opportunity to determine whether he would have received another job offer from a top law firm, and how much he would have made there.

END OF CHAPTER SUMMARY

- Many legal organizations will eschew formal memoranda in favor of shorter, less formal ones.
- If you are writing a less formal memorandum, you should: identify the issue(s); provide a brief summary of the factual situation; and then analyze the respective issues by including application of the facts of your situation to case law. If feasible, include full comparisons as you would in the formal memorandum.
- If you are sending the document by email, do not put the name of the recipient in the send area until you are ready to send it.
- Check for typographical errors.

Grammar Reminders

1. When Micheo & Yoon made the promise, they were essentially....

   Unless you are consciously using the gender-neutral "they," use a singular pronoun for a singular person, place, or thing. An entity that is singular is an "it," not a "they."

2. Courts have held that where a promisee is prevented from obtaining all or most of the benefit of a promise, there is likely a substantial detriment. *Onorato Const., Inc. v. Eastman Const. Co.*, 711 A.2d 1363 (N.J. Super. Ct. App. Div. 1998).

   The writer wrote "courts have held," yet only cited one case. The writer should either string cite or begin the sentence at the word "where."

3. It can be shown that Mr. Li was reasonable to rely on Micheo & Yoon's assurance that he would have a job after graduating law school.

   Passive voice. Begin the sentence at "Mr. Li."

4. Based on precedent/facts/the law, a court is unlikely to hold Micheo & Yoon liable for promissory estoppel.

   What else would the basis be? Just begin with "a court."

5. A page-long paragraph.

   While there may be the occasional need to write a longer paragraph, find ways to break up your paragraphs so that they are readable. Otherwise, it's just cruel.

Brief for Appellant

THIS CASE HAS BEEN SCHEDULED FOR ORAL ARGUMENT
MONTH X–MONTH X, 2024
No. XX-XXXX

IN THE UNITED STATES COURT OF APPEALS
FOR THE THIRD CIRCUIT

Spencer Li,
Plaintiff-Appellant,
v.
Micheo & Yoon,
Defendant-Appellee.

APPEAL FROM THE UNITED STATES DISTRICT COURT
FOR THE DISTRICT OF NEW JERSEY

BRIEF FOR APPELLANT

Mackenzie Ward/
Chandrasekar & Jackson LLP
New Jersey Bar No. 123456
27 Burr Road
Maplewood, New Jersey 07040
201-123-4567

ATTORNEY FOR APPELLANT

STATEMENT OF JURISDICTION

This case states a claim of promissory estoppel pursuant to the RESTATEMENT (SECOND) OF CONTRACTS § 139(1) (Am. Law. Inst. 1981). The United States Court for the District of New Jersey had subject matter jurisdiction over this matter pursuant to 28 U.S.C. § 1332 (2018) because the plaintiff is a legal resident of Delaware and the defendant's place of business is in New Jersey, and the amount in controversy exceeds $75,000. The United States Court of Appeals for the Third Circuit has jurisdiction over this appeal pursuant to 28 U.S.C. § 1291 (2018) because this is an appeal of a final judgment in a civil case. The final order was entered on September 5, 2023, and the notice of appeal was timely filed on October 1, 2023, pursuant to 28 U.S.C. § 2107 (2018).

STATEMENT OF THE ISSUE

Whether, under the requirements for a promissory estoppel claim, Mr. Li reasonably relied on Micheo & Yoon's job offer—which was contingent on the completion of several conditions, which he satisfied—and whether he in fact shifted his position in detriment on the promise, which they subsequently refused to enforce.

STATEMENT OF THE CASE

Statement of Facts

On February 26, 2023, Spencer Li brought a promissory estoppel claim against law firm Micheo & Yoon, who employed him during both summers of law school before revoking their post-graduation, full-time employment offer. R. 1. Micheo & Yoon is a prestigious New Jersey firm, currently ranked 88th on AmFirm 100—a ranking of the top 100 law firms in the country based on salary, annual business, and client satisfaction. R. 26. The firm hired first-year student Mr. Li for its Summer Associate Program where he quickly distinguished himself as an exceptional summer associate. R. 21. In addition to his outstanding work ethic and gregarious personality, he demonstrated excellent research skills: his supervising attorneys noted in their evaluations that Mr. Li had strong research skills and particularly impressive legal analysis abilities. R. 21. Mr. Li worked for the firm during his second-year summer as well, and the firm confirmed that his work was "as outstanding as his first-year performance." R. 22.

Typically, law firm culture mandates that the law students who work at the firm during the second-year summer are extended offers to join the firm after graduation, as long as their work product meets basic requirements. R. 22. According to Micheo & Yoon, occasionally a first-year summer associate is so outstanding that they make a conditional offer for that student to work for them after graduation. R. 22. Mr. Li was in fact that student. R. 22.

At the close of his first-year summer internship, the Director of Attorney Recruiting, Janet Heinan, told Mr. Li that if he (1) maintained a "high G.P.A.," (2) was on journal or moot court, and (3) worked for the firm his second summer, the firm would extend Mr. Li an offer in November of his third year of law school. R. 20. Notably, the firm chose to extend Mr. Li the offer despite there being a moderate economic recession. R. 20. Mr. Li was delighted by this offer as it satisfied his major job criteria: working in big law and remaining in his home state of New Jersey. R. 11. Accordingly, Mr. Li proceeded through law school in reliance on the offer and focused on satisfying the conditions of the promise. R. 12, 14, 16. Subsequently, Mr. Li joined his school's law review editorial staff and had a 3.8 G.P.A. R. 12. Mr. Li was an attractive candidate for many law firms, which would have vied for him to work for them his second summer, but he elected not to interview with other firms because he knew he would be working for Micheo & Yoon after graduation. R. 12, 14. Mr. Li diligently satisfied the conditions of the firm's offer and was therefore confident that he had secured post-graduation employment. R. 16. In reliance on this job offer, Mr. Li elected not to renew his apartment lease, instead choosing to put a down payment on a house, which he found by means of recommendations from Micheo & Yoon associates who lived in the area. R. 28. The house was located on the opposite side of town from Mr. Li's current apartment, closer to the office. R. 28.

In October of his third year of law school, Mr. Li received an email from Ms. Heinan, explaining that Micheo & Yoon would not be able to extend Mr. Li an offer for post-graduation employment due to economic circumstances. R. 17. Because it was late in the hiring process and the dip in the economy had reduced the number of available jobs, Mr. Li's attempt to seek employment at other firms was unsuccessful. R. 18. Ultimately, he found employment with a solo practitioner that paid a salary of $50,000, which is about 25 percent of the $195,000 starting salary for first-year associates at Micheo & Yoon. R. 18, 25. Mr. Li currently has a job in Pennsylvania that pays $100,000. R. 11.

According to Ms. Heinan, the firm typically only offers post-graduation employment to students who are in the top 10 to 15 percent of their class and expects those students to have been on the executive boards of their law school's journal or advocacy team. R. 22. She also asserts, however, that the firm regularly makes exceptions to that "unwritten rule." R. 22. Nevertheless, Ms. Heinan claims that the firm was "disappointed" to learn of the dip in Mr. Li's G.P.A. and his decision not to take on an executive position on journal—neither of which were conditions to their promise of employment. R. 20, 23.

As previously mentioned, at the time Ms. Heinan extended the offer to Mr. Li, there was a recession that impacted law business across the country. R. 27. Micheo & Yoon revoked Mr. Li's offer because of the "economic hit" that the law firm took, which resulted in their reducing their first-year associate offers from twenty-five to twenty-three. R. 24. According to Marcus Johnson, Senior Director of Professional Development, Communications, and Research at the American Association of Law Placement (AALP)—which compiles hiring statistics of law firms nationwide—when Fortune 500 businesses lose money, firms naturally lose work. R. 26. Consequently, "when firms lose work, there are often layoffs, reductions in hiring, or both. Revoking offers is uncommon unless there are extenuating circumstances." R. 27. Importantly, Johnson noted that not all firms bringing in revenue comparable to Micheo & Yoon laid off associates, or even revoked offers; in fact, only about a third of law firms nationwide even reduced the number of new hires. R. 27.

Procedural History

On February 26, 2023, Mr. Li filed a complaint against law firm Micheo & Yoon in the United States District Court for the District of New Jersey seeking a judgment of $95,000 on the theory of promissory estoppel. R. 1. Mr. Li's complaint alleged that he was entitled to relief because he relied to his detriment on Micheo & Yoon's promise of post-graduation employment. R. 1. On March 15, 2023, Micheo & Yoon answered the complaint. R. 12. On June 18, 2023, Micheo & Yoon filed a motion for summary judgment and asked the court to dismiss Mr. Li's complaint. R. 15.

On September 5, 2023, the United States District Court for the District of New Jersey granted Micheo & Yoon's motion for summary judgment, finding that there were no genuine issues of material fact in the dispute. R. 37. The court held that, as a matter of law, Mr. Li failed to meet his burden of establishing promissory estoppel because his reliance on the promise of employment was unreasonable, even though he did incur a detriment. R. 37. Mr. Li appealed the district court's decision to the United States Court of Appeals for the Third Circuit on October 1, 2023. R. 39. On January 3, 2024, the United States Court of Appeals for the Third Circuit certified two issues for appeal: (1) whether Mr. Li reasonably relied on Micheo & Yoon's promise, and (2) whether he in fact shifted his position in detriment on that promise. R. 40.

SUMMARY OF THE ARGUMENT

A law student should be able to rely on the clear promises of future employment with a law firm, particularly when it is reasonable and foreseeable that he will forgo other employment opportunities as a result. This situation falls squarely within the interests that the doctrine of promissory estoppel was created to protect. In New Jersey, in order to succeed on a claim for promissory estoppel, four elements must be satisfied: (1) a clear and definite promise, (2) made with the expectation that the promisee will rely upon it, and (3) reasonable reliance upon the promise, (4) which results in definite and substantial detriment. It is uncontested that Micheo & Yoon made a promise of conditional employment to Spencer Li, with the expectation that he would rely upon it. Mr. Li can successfully demonstrate that the other two elements have been met as well—he was reasonable in his reliance upon the promise, which resulted in detrimental reliance. It was reasonable for Mr. Li to rely on Micheo & Yoon's promise of employment because Mr. Li consulted industry standard to inform his decision to rely on the promise, met all the necessary conditions to the offer, and Micheo & Yoon maintained sole discretion over the promise, which was substantially certain to mature within several months.

It is uncommon to revoke an offer unless there are "extenuating circumstances." The moderate economic recession, which had been a background factor present since the beginning of Mr. Li and Micheo & Yoon's relationship, does not constitute an extenuating circumstance; therefore, it was reasonable for Mr. Li to rely on the offer, without fear that his offer may suddenly be rescinded. Next, Mr. Li met all of the conditions necessary to the offer of employment: he (1) maintained a high G.P.A., (2) joined his law journal's editorial staff, and (3) came back to work for the firm his second summer. Mr. Li can demonstrate that he did in fact maintain a "high" G.P.A. because he remained on the Dean's List—an academic distinction recognizing high academic achievement—throughout law school. Next, it was reasonable for Mr. Li to rely on the promise because Micheo & Yoon had complete discretion and control over the offer, and did not act fairly in communicating their decision to rescind Mr. Li's offer last minute. While the firm does not have superior control over external influences such as the state of the economy, they knew that was a factor for several years, but reneged on his offer just months before it was expected to mature, leaving Mr. Li with a poor chance of finding alternative employment of the same caliber. Finally, Mr. Li completed the final condition to his promise—working for the firm his second summer—and expected the offer to mature in just a few months. He had negotiated the material terms of his employment and made living arrangements accordingly, substantially certain that the offer was soon to mature. Based on the foregoing, it is clear that Mr. Li's reliance on Micheo & Yoon's promise of future employment was reasonable.

To establish the final element for a promissory estoppel claim, the court must determine whether the plaintiff suffered a substantial hardship or injustice in reasonable reliance on the promise. The court considers whether the plaintiff has incurred a definite detriment and a substantial detriment. Mr. Li suffered detriment of a definite nature as he experienced a reduction in expected salary from $195,000 at Micheo & Yoon to $100,000 at the Pennsylvania firm where he currently works. He also incurred additional, external costs in reliance on Micheo & Yoon's representations regarding the job offer: he declined to renew his old lease, put a down payment on a house in a new area of the city close to the Micheo & Yoon office, and gave up opportunities for employment with other big law firms in reliance on their promise of employment. Mr. Li can also show that his reliance amounted to a substantial change in position, thus satisfying the second component of detrimental reliance. Mr. Li forfeited other employment opportunities in reliance on his reasonable understanding that he had successfully secured employment with Micheo & Yoon. Mr. Li was unable to receive the expected benefits of the promise: he received none of the benefit of the promise of post-graduation employment at Micheo & Yoon as he never had the opportunity to even begin working there as a first-year associate. He also lost two summers of potential networking with other firms, suffered a considerable reduction in expected salary, and ended up having to move to Pennsylvania to find employment.

Mr. Li has a valid promissory estoppel claim in this case because he can show that he relied reasonably on Micheo & Yoon's conditional promise of employment, and in fact suffered a definite and substantial detriment. The doctrine of promissory estoppel will be enforced when there is no other means to avoid injustice, such as in the case at bar.

ARGUMENT AND CITATIONS OF AUTHORITIES

I. Mr. Li's reliance on Micheo & Yoon's promise of post-graduation employment was reasonable and he did in fact suffer a definite and substantial detriment as a result of such reliance meaning; accordingly, Mr. Li can support a prima facie claim for promissory estoppel.

The essential justification for the theory of promissory estoppel is "the avoidance of substantial hardship or injustice were the promise not to be enforced." *Malaker Corp. Stockholders Protective Comm. v. First Jersey Nat'l Bank*, 163 N.J. Super. 463, 484, 395 A.2d 222, 232 (Super. Ct. App. Div. 1978). Promissory estoppel is a remedy by which a promisee may seek redress when a promisor should reasonably expect his promise to induce forbearance or action on the part of the promisee. RESTATEMENT (SECOND) OF CONTRACTS § 139(1) (Am. Law Inst. 1981). The equitable doctrine of promissory estoppel may be invoked in situations where there is no enforceable agreement between the parties and where justice would be served by enforcing the promise. *Carlson v. Arnot-Ogden Mem'l Hosp.*, 918 F.2d 411, 416 (3d Cir. 1990).

The appellate court reviews orders granting summary judgment *de novo* to determine whether genuine issues of material fact would preclude summary judgment. *Lucent Info. Mgmt., Inc. v. Lucent Tech. Inc.*, 186 F.3d 311, 315 (3d Cir. 1999). The reviewing court applies the same test that the district court applied in the first instance. *Petruzzi's IGA Supermarkets, Inc. v. Darling-Delaware Co.*, 998 F.2d 1224, 1230 (3d Cir. 1993). In determining whether summary judgment is warranted, the court views the record and draws inferences in a light most favorable to the non-moving party, which in the present case is Mr. Li. Fed. R. Civ. P. 56(c); *see Arnold M. Diamond, Inc. v. Gulf Coast Trailing Co.*, 180 F.3d 518, 521 (3d Cir. 1999).

In New Jersey, a plaintiff may recover under a promissory estoppel claim where the following criteria are met: (1) a clear and definite promise, (2) made with the expectation that the promisee will rely upon it, and (3) reasonable reliance upon the promise, (4) which results in definite and substantial detriment. *Pop's Cones, Inc. v. Resorts Intern. Hotel, Inc.*, 704 A.2d 1321, 1323 (N.J. Super. Ct. App. Div. 1998) (adopting § 90 of the RESTATEMENT (SECOND) OF CONTRACTS). It is undisputed that Micheo & Yoon's offer constituted a clear and definite promise and was made with the expectation that Mr. Li would rely upon it. Mr. Li has provided sufficient evidence to demonstrate that he acted reasonably in relying upon the promise of employment and incurred definite and substantial detriment in the form of lost wages and lost opportunity to find employment elsewhere. Therefore, we respectfully request that this Court reverse the District Court's judgment for the Appellee.

A. Mr. Li's reliance on Micheo & Yoon's offer was reasonable because he complied with industry standard, properly satisfied all of the conditions of the promise, and relied on the promisor who exercised full control and discretion over a promise that was substantially certain to mature.

To satisfy the third element of a claim for promissory estoppel, a plaintiff must show that he reasonably relied on a representation made by defendant, which induced him to abandon an existing right or influenced him to act or refrain from acting. *Friedman v. Tappan Dev. Corp.*, 126 A.2d 646, 653 (N.J. 1956). The reliance must be "reasonable and justifiable," and the burden of proof rests on the party asserting the estoppel. *Foley Mach. Co. v. Amland Contractors, Inc.*, 209 N.J. Super. 70, 75–76 (App. Div. 1986). The promissory estoppel approach applies to future promises and is a flexible and well-established doctrine. *Id.*; *Malaker*, 395 A.2d at 230 ("Suffice it to say that given an appropriate case, the doctrine [of promissory estoppel] will be enforced."). Because promissory estoppel rests on principles of fairness, courts typically treat the requirement of reasonable reliance as a question of fact reserved for the fact finder. *See Friedman*, 126 A.2d at 646; RESTATEMENT, CONTRACTS 2D, § 90.

In determining whether the plaintiff's reliance on a promise was reasonable, courts consider several factors, including predominant industry standard, whether the promisee successfully completed the conditions to the promise, sole discretion or control over the promise, and whether the promise is substantially certain to occur. *SASCO 1997 NI,*

LLC v. Zudkewich, 767 A.2d 469, 478 (N.J. 2001) (holding that courts consult industry norms in determining what is reasonable); *Royal Assocs. v. Concannon*, 490 A.2d 357, 357 (N.J. Super. Ct. App. Div. 1985) (holding that completing the conditions to a promise render a promisee's reliance reasonable); *Pop's Cones*, 704 A.2d at 1322 (holding that where the promisor maintained full control of the premises to which the promisee expected to relocate and sole discretion over revocation of the offer, the promisee was reasonable in relying on the promise); *In re Phillips Petroleum Sec. Litig.*, 881 F.2d 1236, 1250 (3d Cir. 1989) (holding that courts are inclined to find reliance reasonable where the offer is substantially certain to mature).

New Jersey courts often use industry practice to determine what is reasonable. *SASCO*, 767 A.2d at 478; *Thomas v. Princeton Univ.*, No. A-0680-14T1, 2016 N.J. Super. Unpub. LEXIS 2515, at *10 (Super. Ct. App. Div. Nov. 23, 2016). In *SASCO*, which arose from a dispute over a loan transfer, the predominant industry practice pertinent to the case was to wait until judgment to conduct an asset search. 767 A.2d at 478. The court held that the plaintiff, SASCO, was reasonable in relying on this practice, which was dominant throughout the industry. *Id.* at 477. Alternatively, in *Thomas*, the court held that a term employee's reliance on a promise of future permanent employment was unreasonable, primarily because of the employee's temporary status as a construction manager. 2016 N.J. Super. Unpub. LEXIS 2515 at *10. While the promisee allegedly expressed his desire to become a permanent employee, there is not an established industry practice dictating that workers who are hired for specific construction projects are typically offered regular employment after the completion of their project. *Id.* at *3. The court held that it was unreasonable for the term employee to rely on his employer's promise to consider the possibility of regular employment. *Id.* While New Jersey courts often use industry practice to determine what is reasonable, that alone cannot justify relying on an offer that explicitly instructs the promisee not to rely on it. *Fletcher-Harlee Corp. v. Pote Concrete Contrs.*, Inc., 482 F.3d 247, 249 (3d Cir. 2007). In *Fletcher-Harlee*, the subcontractor expressly disclaimed his intention to be bound and the general contractor failed to allege anything that would render his reliance on the subcontractor's submission reasonable. *Id.* at 250–51.

In New Jersey, courts have recognized reasonable reliance where the promisee has successfully met all of the necessary conditions to a promise. *Royal Assocs.*, 490 A.2d at 357; *Watson v. City of Salem*, 934 F. Supp. 643, 660 (D.N.J. 1995) (holding that a plaintiff's promissory estoppel claim failed because the plaintiff failed to successfully complete the background investigation, which was a valid condition precedent to the enforcement of the promise). In *Royal Associates*, the tenant purchased a dog in reliance on the promise of the landlord that if he were to purchase a dog, the dog would be permitted on the premises. 490 A.2d at 359. The court proscribed the eviction of the tenant for allegedly violating a "no pets clause" in the lease. *Id.* at 360. The court held that the tenant reasonably relied on the landlord's promise to let them keep their dog because they properly satisfied the conditions of the landlord's promise. *Id.* Conversely, courts are unlikely to find reasonable reliance if the promisee has failed to satisfy the conditions to the promise. *Bonczek v. Carter-Wallace, Inc.*, 701 A.2d 742, 744–46 (N.J. Super. Ct. App. Div. 1997). In *Bonczek*, the plaintiff potential employee's offer of employment was contingent upon the completion of satisfactory reference checks, which the plaintiff failed to complete as a result of embellishments regarding his prior title and salary that raised questions about his credibility and character. *Id.* at 745. The court denied the plaintiff's promissory estoppel claim, holding that it was not reasonable for the plaintiff to rely on the promise of employment given that he had failed to satisfy the requisite conditions of the promise. *Id.*

Courts are more likely to find it was reasonable for the promisee to rely on the promise when the promisor has sole discretion to back out of the promise, or the circumstances are within the control of the promisor. *Pop's Cones*, 704 A.2d at 1322; *Peck v. Imedia, Inc.*, 679 A.2d 745, 753 (Super. Ct. App. Div. 1996) (holding that an employee acted reasonably in relying on an offer for full-time employment because the rescission of the offer was based solely on the employer's changing his mind about the employee's "fit"). In *Pop's Cones*, the court found that the plaintiff, a store owner, lost its prior location in reliance on the defendant's promise that the plaintiff could relocate its business to the defendant's location. 704 A.2d at 1323. The plaintiff could have relocated to a different location or waited to relocate if not for the defendant's offer, which it repudiated once the plaintiff was already in the process of relocating. *Id.* The defendant having full control over the premises and the circumstances surrounding the plaintiff's move, its waiting to notify the store owner until relocation was already occurring, and the fact that it was in the defendant's sole discretion to back out of the offer—which it did—supported the finding that the store owner was reasonable in relying on the promise. *Id.* at 1326. Similarly, in *Peck*, the plaintiff alleged that she continued to complete work as an independent contractor for the defendant and advise clients of her decision to close her business and move to a different city in reliance on this job offer before defendants notified her that her offer of employment had already been terminated. 679 A.2d at 753. The court reasoned that the plaintiff should be permitted to proceed on her promissory estoppel claim because defendants did not act fairly or timely in communicating their decision to rescind her job offer. *Id.* Her losses flowed from the defendant's lack of good faith and fair dealing "attributable to [the defendant's] delay in expressing the decision to terminate the relationship." *Id.*

Alternatively, when the promisor has no control over an external factor, such as unpredictable statewide budget cuts, a court may find that it was unreasonable for the promisee to rely on the promise. *E. Orange Bd. of Educ. v. N.J. Sch. Const. Corp.*, 963 A.2d 865, 874–75 (N.J. Super. Ct. App. Div. 2009). In *E. Orange Board*, the court held that there was no viable claim because the plaintiff Board of Education failed to demonstrate reasonable reliance on a commitment that all or some of its school facilities projects would be funded and constructed during a specific time frame. *Id.* at 874. In addition, the court noted that the promisor did not revoke or repeal the approval of any of the eligible projects; they "merely deferred their construction because of the critical shortage of capital funding." *Id.*

Courts are inclined to find reliance reasonable where the offer is substantially certain to mature. *In re Phillips*, 881 F.2d at 1250 ("reliance upon a mere expression of future intention" cannot be considered reasonable); *Goldfarb v. Solimine*, No. A-3740-16T2, 2019 N.J. Super. Unpub. LEXIS 1472, at *6–7 (Super. Ct. App. Div. June 26, 2019) (holding that it was reasonable for the plaintiff to quit his job in reliance on the defendant's promise of immediate employment, and awarded damages based on the difference between his actual earnings and the base salary the defendant promised). For instance, in *Schley v. Microsoft Corp.*, No. 08-3589 (DRD), 2008 U.S. Dist. LEXIS 96059, at *13–14 (D.N.J. Nov. 24, 2008), the plaintiff received a written offer, negotiated compensation and benefits extensively, and was induced to purchase a new home and quit his previous job immediately. The court held that it was reasonable for the plaintiff to rely on the employment offer because the promise was near fruition and there were no material conditions left to negotiate. *Id.*

Alternatively, if the promise is not expected to mature until far into the future or the terms of the offer are still in the early stages of negotiation, a court may not find it reasonable for the promisee to rely on the promise. *Thomas*, 2016 N.J. Super. Unpub. LEXIS 2515, at *3–4. For example, the term employee in *Thomas* failed to demonstrate reasonable reliance on the alleged promise of future permanent employment in part because the offer was expected to materialize at an unascertained point in the future, and he conceded that his employer had agreed only to consider making such an offer. *Id.* Because no extensive negotiations had occurred and the promise was to transpire at a distant point in time, there was no reasonable reliance. *Id.*

Mr. Li relied reasonably on the conditional promise made by Micheo & Yoon as his decision was guided by ordinary industry standard. The revocation of offers to new hires is not a common practice for law firm businesses. R.23. As Marcus Johnson of the AALP points out, "Revoking offers is uncommon unless there are extenuating circumstances." R. 27. A moderate economic recession that has persisted for several years does not constitute an "extenuating circumstance," rendering the revocation of Mr. Li's employment offer unusual in the legal industry. Mr. Li reasonably relied on his knowledge of the ordinary industry standard—taking into account the recession, he understood that when firms lose work, there are often layoffs and/or reductions in hiring. R. 27. While he may have expected that the firm would reduce the number of hires, or even lay people off because of the recession, he had no reason to suspect that his long-standing offer would be revoked. Given that New Jersey courts consult relevant industry norms in determining what is reasonable, *SASCO*, 767 A.2d at 478, and Micheo & Yoon never expressly directed Mr. Li not to rely on their offer which would invalidate reliance, *Fletcher-Harlee*, 482 F.3d at 249, it follows that Mr. Li was reasonable in relying on their offer of employment to his detriment. Unlike the term employee in *Thomas*, 2016 N.J. Super. Unpub. LEXIS 2515, at *3, who was a temporary worker whose employment would naturally terminate after the completion of the single project he was hired to manage, the nature of Mr. Li's employment follows from a completely different, well-established industry practice. In accordance with typical law firm culture, Mr. Li's working for the firm his second-year results almost automatically in permanent employment. R. 22. Moreover, his employer did not promise to consider him for regular employment, such as the employer in *Thomas*, 2016 N.J. Super. Unpub. LEXIS 2515 at *3, agreed to, but unambiguously offered him full-time employment.

Mr. Li has fulfilled all three of the conditions set forth by Micheo & Yoon in their promise of post-graduation employment: Mr. Li (1) maintained a high G.P.A., (2) joined his law journal's editorial staff, and (3) came back to work for the firm his second summer. R. 12, 16. Mr. Li's successfully completing the conditions necessary to Micheo & Yoon's promise tilts in favor of the Court recognizing reasonable reliance in the present case. Like the plaintiff tenant in *Royal Associates*, 490 A.2d at 357, Mr. Li complied with all the conditions of the promise. That Mr. Li was on journal and came back to the firm for his second summer is unequivocal, notwithstanding the firm's claim that they were "disappointed" that he did not elect to take a position on journal. R.23. Mr. Li was on journal as was required by Micheo & Yoon's offer but did not attempt to become part of the executive board, which was *not* one of the conditions of the firm's offer. R. 16. Because the workload on journal was intense, Mr. Li chose to participate in other extracurriculars, in addition to being on journal, in order to strengthen his skillset as a well-rounded student. R. 16.

Additionally, while Mr. Li's G.P.A. dipped in his second year, he graduated with impressive credentials, maintaining the G.P.A. necessary to make the Dean's List. R. 16. The Dean's List is an academic distinction used to recognize a high level of scholarship and academic excellence. It therefore follows that Mr. Li's G.P.A.—which has always qualified for the Dean's List—constitutes a "high" G.P.A. sufficient to satisfy Micheo & Yoon's third condition. Moreover, Ms. Heinan admits that the firm frequently makes exceptions to the "informal rule" that they prefer students in the top 15 percent of the class. R. 22. Even more, there is no evidence to suggest that Mr. Li was privy to this information, which may have informed his decisions regarding his extracurricular and academic affairs, had he been aware of this informal rule. Lastly, Micheo & Yoon hired Mr. Li for a second summer and commended his performance as being "as outstanding as last year," neglecting to express any concern regarding his slightly lower G.P.A. R. 22. Unlike the plaintiff in *Bonczek*,

701 A.2d at 745, who failed to pass the reference checks contingent to his employment offer, Mr. Li successfully met the three conditions of his employment offer.

It was reasonable for Mr. Li to rely on the firm's promise because Micheo & Yoon had sole discretion over the execution of the offer and exercised superior control over the situation. Like the casino in *Pop's Cones*, 704 A.2d at 1326, who had full control of the premises that the promisee expected to relocate to and sole discretion to retract the offer, Micheo & Yoon had full control over the status of Mr. Li's employment offer and sole discretion to retract the offer. Like the defendants in *Peck*, 679 A.2d at 753, Micheo & Yoon did not act fairly in communicating their decision to rescind Mr. Li's job offer. The moderate recession had been going on for several years, but the firm never expressed to Mr. Li that there was any reason for him to worry about his offer potentially being revoked, or advised him to consider alternative employment options. Instead, during their decision-making process of reneging on offers and other hiring/firing decisions, Micheo & Yoon deliberately left Mr. Li grossly uninformed of the potentiality of his losing his job offer. Even if the firm had notified Mr. Li just months—if not weeks—earlier, Mr. Li could have had a much stronger chance of finding alternative employment. Like the plaintiff in *Peck*, 679 A.2d at 753, Mr. Li's losses resulted from his potential employer's lack of good faith and fair dealing attributable to their delay in communicating their decision to terminate the offer.

While the firm does not have total control over external influences such as the state of the economy, it is significant that the firm was aware of the recession at the very time they made the initial promise to Mr. Li. R. 27. The moderate recession in this case is distinguishable from unexpected budget cuts, such as that in *E. Orange Board*, 963 A.2d at 874–75, which the promisor had no control over or knowledge of beforehand—the firm knew they were in a recession and made hiring decisions accordingly. Even more, Marcus Johnson of the AALP stated that only about a third of law businesses across the country reduced the number of hires they expected as a result of the recession. R. 27. Micheo & Yoon had ample time to discuss the recession's impact on their business, make subsequent hiring and layoff decisions, and notify those whom such decisions affected. Ms. Heinan notified Mr. Li of the revocation years after the recession began, only a month before his offer was due to mature. R. 17, 24.

The logistics of Mr. Li's offer were sufficiently definite in nature, making it reasonable for him to rely on the offer maturing as expected. While the promise of employment may have initially been made two years in advance, the validity of the promise was reinforced when Mr. Li completed his second summer with Micheo & Yoon, where "his work was as outstanding as his first-year performance." R. 22. Given that law firm culture dictates that students who work at the firm during the second-year summer are typically extended offers to join the firm after graduation, the promise of employment extended to Mr. Li was effectively renewed going into his third year of law school, just months before he expected the formal offer to be made in November of his third year. Like the plaintiff in *Schley*, 2008 U.S. Dist. LEXIS 96059, at *13–14, who had negotiated most of the terms of his employment, purchased a home, and left his previous job, Mr. Li had negotiated the material terms of his employment, made living arrangements contingent on the offer, and forgone alternative employment opportunities. R. 12, 16, 22. While Mr. Li did not have to move cities, he was induced to make a down payment on a house in reliance on the firm's offer and gave up his prior apartment lease. R. 28. Mr. Li did so only because he was confident that he would have a stable job with the firm. He discussed these plans and asked for guidance from several of the associates at Micheo & Yoon who he had fostered connections with over his two summers. R. 28. Distinguishable from the term employee in *Thomas*, 2016 N.J. Super. Unpub. LEXIS 2515 at *3–4, who relied unreasonably on a promise to potentially make an offer at some unspecified point in time, Mr. Li relied reasonably on an express promise to offer him employment in the near future, just months after he had fulfilled the third condition to the promise. R. 20, 22.

It was reasonable for Mr. Li to rely on Micheo & Yoon's promise of employment because Mr. Li he acted in accordance with and relied upon industry standard to inform his choice to rely on the promise, he satisfied all of the necessary conditions to the offer of employment, and Micheo & Yoon maintained sole discretion over the promise, which was substantially certain to mature in just several months' time.

B. Mr. Li incurred a definite and substantial detriment in reliance on Micheo & Yoon's promise because he sacrificed many other viable opportunities with other firms, experienced a considerable reduction in expected salary, and incurred substantial moving and housing expenses.

To satisfy the final element for a promissory estoppel claim, a plaintiff must show that he relied on a defendant's promise to his detriment, which can only be avoided by the enforcement of the promise. *Malaker*, 395 A.2d at 228. The plaintiff must demonstrate that the detriment suffered was of a substantial and definite nature, which is a question of fact. *Id.*

The promisee must incur some external, additional cost in reliance on the defendant's representations to satisfy the detrimental reliance element for a viable claim for promissory estoppel. *Kaufman v. Mellon Nat'l Bank & Tr. Co.*, 366 F.2d 326, 332 (3d Cir. 1966); *Peck*, 679 A.2d at 753; *Taylor v. Lincare, Inc.*, No. 15-6284 (RMB/JS), 2016 U.S. Dist. LEXIS 91924, at *35–36 (D.N.J. July 15, 2016) ("In essence, a plaintiff must allege that he sustained 'losses incident to the reliance upon the job offer itself,' such as relocating, incurring moving expenses, giving up clients, or other costs undertaken because of the job offer or promise of continued employment."). For example, in *Peck*, the court found that the plaintiff suffered "obvious detriment" in her reliance on the defendant's promise of full-time employment. *Peck*, 679 A.2d at 753 (quoting *Swider v. Ha-Lo Indus.*, 134 F. Supp. 2d 607, 620 (D.N.J. 2001)). The plaintiff rented out her apartment in Massachusetts, signed a new lease for an apartment in New Jersey, arranged for movers, and gave up her clients in the Boston area. *Id.* at 158. Importantly, the *Peck* court noted that there may be "losses incident to reliance upon the job offer itself that will support a claim for promissory estoppel." *Swider*, 134 F. Supp. 2d at 620.

A promisee must show that the costs undertaken because of the job offer, such as moving expenses, were in fact sustained specifically in reliance on the offer. *See Thomas*, 2016 N.J. Super. Unpub. LEXIS 2515, at *3. For example, in *Thomas*, the court held that the defendant employer's promise to consider hiring the term employee full-time and expressing to the employee the "possibility of regular employment" was insufficient to constitute definite detriment. *Id.* The employee was interested in a permanent position with the defendant, primarily because he would be moving from Maryland to New Jersey, where the defendant was located. *Id.* The employee was already moving regardless of the defendant's offer, and therefore was unable to prove definite detriment on the alleged promise. *Id.*

Moreover, simply passing up another job offer is generally insufficient to demonstrate detrimental reliance of a definite nature. *Swider*, 134 F. Supp. 2d at 620; *Moore v. Merrill Lynch, Pierce, Fenner & Smith, Inc.*,

Civil No. 90-1182 (CSF), 1991 U.S. Dist. LEXIS 10628, at *19 (D.N.J. July 23, 1991); *Ankerstjerne v. Schlumberger Ltd.*, No. 03-3607, 2004 U.S. Dist. LEXIS 9927 (E.D. Pa. 2004) (affirmed by *Ankerstjerne v. Schlumberger, Ltd.*, 155 F. App'x 48 (3d Cir. 2005)) (noting that courts have refused to recognize damages for "roads not taken." Courts have found that "refraining from pursuing other employment opportunities altogether is not a sufficient detriment to support a promissory estoppel claim."); *Jayne v. Archdiocese of Phila.*, No. 93-4039, 1994 U.S. Dist. LEXIS 3810, *3–4 (E.D. Pa. Mar. 25, 1994) (holding that "[plaintiff's] failure to seek other employment is not forbearance of a definite and substantial character as a matter of law"). In *Swider*, the plaintiff alleged that he passed up another job offer in reliance on the defendant potential employer's alleged oral promises. 134 F. Supp. 2d at 620. The court held that the plaintiff's alleged detrimental reliance was inadequate because the plaintiff did not inform the defendant of the other offer, or his decision to turn it down in favor of his position with the defendant. *Id.* Similarly, in *Moore*, the plaintiff failed to show that there was detrimental reliance or forbearance of another position based on any promise of employment with the defendant, Merrill Lynch. 1991 U.S. Dist. LEXIS 10628 at *19. Even accepting the plaintiff's assertion that she sacrificed another life-time employment offer for the Merrill Lynch position, the court held that because she never pleaded that she told the defendant that she had this other offer and "was on the fence," the reliance element was missing. *Id.*

Additionally, the promisee must demonstrate a "substantial change in position" in order to satisfy the detrimental reliance element. *Kaufman v. Mellon Nat'l Bank & Tr. Co.*, 366 F.2d 326, 333 (3d Cir. 1966); *Johnson v. Dunkin' Donuts Franchising L.L.C.*, Civil Action No. 11-1117, 2014 U.S. Dist. LEXIS 88446, at *14 (W.D. Pa. June 30, 2014); *Shebar v. Sanyo Bus. Sys. Corp.*, 544 A.2d 377, 380 (N.J. 1988). In *Shebar*, the plaintiff revoked his acceptance of an offer of employment from Sony as a result of a meeting with defendant Sanyo and reliance on the assurances made to him in that meeting. 544 A.2d at 380. Because the plaintiff informed the defendant that he rejected the job opportunity he had secured at Sony and the defendant acknowledged such, the court held that the plaintiff had established substantial detriment. *Id.* at 383. The court found that forfeiting one job in reliance on another amounts to a substantial change of position. *Id.* Alternatively, in *Johnson*, the court held that the plaintiff failed to show substantial detriment because it did not undergo a substantial change in position. 2014 U.S. Dist. LEXIS 88446, at *71. While the plaintiff argued that it did in fact undergo a substantial change in position by continuing development of the construction site with the belief that it would become a Dunkin' store, the court rejected this claim because the plaintiffs failed to provide any evidence regarding "precisely what development activities were complete after the promises were purportedly made by Dunkin'." *Id.* at *70. Further, the court held, the evidence proffered demonstrated that they intended to develop the site regardless of the alleged deal with Dunkin', meaning that the preparatory work done on the property would have been completed regardless of the defendant's alleged promise. *Id.* at *71. Even more, the plaintiffs presented no evidence to suggest they had any alternative development opportunities that they refrained from pursuing because of negotiations with Dunkin' or that they acted any differently because of the defendant's promises. *Id.*

Moreover, for a plaintiff to prove he has incurred a substantial detriment on a conditional offer, he must show that he took substantial steps to perform the necessary condition prior to enforcement leading to a substantial change in position. *Kaufman*, 366 F.2d at 332. In *Kaufman*, the defendant construction company's promise was made on the condition that the plaintiff lenders would take definite action of a substantial character by entering into a contract to purchase the property at issue, but they failed to do so. *Id.* Instead, they took no action that in any way altered their position adversely and there was no recorded evidence to suggest that the plaintiffs incurred any expense, made any additional investment, or suffered any actual loss as a result of their alleged reliance on the defendant's promise. *Id.* at 332–33.

If a promisee is unable to enjoy the entire benefit—or at least a considerable amount of the benefit—of a promise, then the court is likely to find a substantial detriment. *Pop's Cones*, 704 A.2d at 1323. For example, in *Pop's Cones*, the plaintiff lost its prior store location and never benefitted from the defendant casino's promise to provide the new location to the store owner because the defendant rescinded its promise while the plaintiff was in the midst of moving. *Id.* The court held that the store incurred substantial detriment in reliance on the promise of the defendant because they lost their prior location and never benefitted from use of the promised location. *Id.* The plaintiff could have relocated to a different location or waited to relocate if not for the defendant's offer, which it repudiated once the plaintiff was already in the process of relocating. *Id.*

Alternatively, if a promisee receives most of the benefits of a promise, there is likely not enough of a loss to constitute substantial detriment. *Sadej v. Arturi*, No. A-1424-16T1, 2019 N.J. Super. Unpub. LEXIS 1043, at *28 (Super. Ct. App. Div. May 7, 2019); *Pane v. RCA Corp.*, 868 F.2d 631, 638 (3d Cir. 1989) (holding that the plaintiff failed to show detrimental reliance because the alleged detriment he incurred from purchasing stocks and the anxiety it produced could have been alleviated by selling his stock for a profit). In *Sadej*, the Sadejs obtained approvals to construct improvements to the existing residence and garage. 2019 N.J. Super. Unpub. LEXIS 1043, at *19. About eight months later, a stop work order was issued to the Sadejs for "lost zoning approval" when they had completed approximately 80 percent of the improvements. *Id.* at *2. The court held that there was no significant detriment because the Sadejs were able to complete most of their improvements (besides attaching the garage), and there was no evidence regarding the value the improvement to the garage would have added to the property; moreover, there was no evidence of how they intended to use the improved space . *Id.* at *24.

Mr. Li can show that he has suffered a detriment of a definite and substantial nature in reliance on the promise made by Micheo & Yoon. Mr. Li can show that, as a result of his reasonable reliance on their offer, he has suffered definite losses—incurring moving expenses and forgoing alternative employment—and substantial lost wages from accepting a different job, which paid a salary that was 25 percent of the starting salary at Micheo & Yoon.

Mr. Li suffered a definite detriment regarding a reduction in expected salary from $195,000 at Micheo & Yoon to $100,000 at the Pennsylvania firm where he currently works. R. 11. Conservatively, Mr. Li is suing for $95,000 to recover the difference in salary, although he can show that he incurred additional, external costs in reliance on Micheo & Yoon's representations regarding the job offer. Like the plaintiff in *Peck*, 679 A.2d at 753, who suffered "obvious detriment" by renting out her apartment, signing a new lease, hiring movers, and giving up clients in reliance on her future employer's promise of employment, Mr. Li refrained from renewing his old lease, put a down payment on a house in a new area of the city close to his expected office building, and gave up opportunities for employment with other big law firms in reliance on Micheo & Yoon's promise of employment. R. 28. As the *Peck* court noted, Mr. Li in fact suffered losses "incident to reliance upon the job offer itself [which] support a claim for promissory estoppel" against Micheo & Yoon. 679 A.2d at 753. Mr. Li can show that the detriment he incurred was a direct result of his reliance on Micheo & Yoon's promise. Mr. Li elected not to interview with other firms solely because he already had an attractive offer from Micheo & Yoon. R. 14. Given that Micheo & Yoon was one of the most prestigious law firms in New Jersey and Mr. Li had already spent his first summer fostering connections with the firm's team, this was an exceptional offer for Mr. Li, who had no reservations about acting on the offer and accepting the position. R. 11. Unlike the term employee in *Thomas*, 2016 N.J. Super. Unpub. LEXIS 2515, at *3, who was moving cities irrespective of the defendant employer's alleged promise of full-time employment, Mr. Li put the down payment on the house and arranged to move out of his current apartment in direct reliance on the firm's offer of employment. Mr. Li reasonably expected that he would remain in New Jersey for long enough to make it worth investing in a house, and chose the area based on the firm's location. He can therefore prove definite detriment on the offer.

Mr. Li did not simply forgo another job offer without notifying Micheo & Yoon. Rather, Mr. Li deliberately committed to working full-time after graduation at Micheo & Yoon. Not only did he dedicate both of his summers to working for the firm and building meaningful connections with the associates, but he also communicated to the firm that he was forgoing other employment in reliance on their offer of post-graduation employment. While the facts may not reveal that Mr. Li expressly articulated to the firm that he was forgoing potential alternative employment, it is clear from his decision to work at the firm for his second summer that he was planning to do so—working there his second summer was one of the conditions Mr. Li was required to complete in order for the promise of employment to mature. R. 14, 20. The plaintiffs in *Swider*, 134 F. Supp. 2d at 620, and *Moore*, 1991 U.S. Dist. LEXIS 10628 at *19, failed to show that there was detrimental reliance or forbearance of another employment offer based on a promise from the defendant. Conversely, Micheo & Yoon knew that Mr. Li was a strong candidate and that many top-tier firms were interested in hiring him. R. 12. Mr. Li, however, was pleased with his offer from Micheo & Yoon as it satisfied his job criteria—working in big law and remaining in his home state of New Jersey—and was therefore comfortable relying on their offer and forgoing alternative options. R. 11. That the firm knew that he turned down alternative employment in favor of the position with Micheo & Yoon supports Mr. Li's ability to show detrimental reliance.

Mr. Li can satisfactorily show that his reliance amounted to a "substantial change in position," thus satisfying the second component of the element of detrimental reliance. Mr. Li forfeited other employment opportunities in reliance on his reasonable understanding that he had successfully secured employment with Micheo & Yoon. R. 14, 16. The plaintiff in *Shebar* demonstrated a substantial change in position by rejecting a job opportunity with Sony in reliance on the offer from the defendant employer. 544 A.2d at 380. Analogously, Mr. Li rejected interviewing with firms that would have vied for him in reliance on the offer from Micheo & Yoon. R. 12, 14. Mr. Li had already spent a summer with the firm and was confident that the firm was an excellent fit for him; he thereby rejected to interview elsewhere in reliance on the defendant's promise to employ him. R. 14, 16. Conversely, in *Johnson*, the plaintiffs failed to demonstrate substantial reliance in their continued development of a property because they were unable to show what work had been completed after the promises were allegedly made to induce such action and the evidence showed they planned to continue construction regardless of the promise. 2014 U.S. Dist. LEXIS 88446 at *70. *Johnson*, *id.*, is distinguishable from the instant case, where Mr. Li can affirmatively show what actions he has taken after the promise from Micheo & Yoon was made: Mr. Li put a down payment on a house, declined to renew his current lease, and was relocating to a different area of the city. R. 28. Further, it is clear that he would not have taken such action regardless of the promise. While it was unclear whether the plaintiffs in *Johnson*, 2014 U.S. Dist. LEXIS 88446, at *70, acted differently because of the defendant's promises, it is undeniable that Mr. Li acted differently in incurring moving and housing-related expenses in reliance on Micheo & Yoon's offer.

Further, if the alleged offer was conditional, the promisee must show that he took substantial steps to perform the necessary condition prior to enforcement, *Kaufman*, 366 F.2d at 332, which Mr. Li can demonstrate: he completed the three express conditions necessary to the firm's offer. R. 12, 16, 22. It is clear that Mr. Li took action in a way that altered his position adversely—he incurred expenses and made an additional investment by putting a down payment on a house since he expected to remain in his home state for the foreseeable future and expected to have a reliable income to support this financial decision. He therefore clearly suffered an actual loss in lost wages and incurred expenses related to his financial investment in a permanent home.

Mr. Li was unable to receive the expected benefits of the promise. Mr. Li received none of the benefit of the promise of post-graduation employment at Micheo & Yoon as he never had the opportunity to even begin working there as a first-year associate. R. 20, 24. In addition to losing the primary expected benefit of long-term employment at Micheo & Yoon, Mr. Li concomitantly lost two summers of potential networking with other firms, suffered a considerable reduction in expected salary, and ended up having to settle for employment in Pennsylvania. R. 17, 25. While it could be argued that Mr. Li's two summers interning for Micheo & Yoon constitute a benefit in providing him with meaningful work experience, any benefit he may have received from that is overshadowed by the fact that his offer was subsequently revoked. In light of typical law firm culture, it hurts Mr. Li more to have to explain why his offer from a firm that he worked for both summers was rescinded than it helps him to have those two years of work experience. The salary reduction that Mr. Li experienced—from the expected $195,000 to $50,000 working for a solo practitioner rather than a big law firm as he hoped—constituted a considerable loss, especially considering the persistence of the economic recession. R. 18. Despite the fact that he was eventually able to obtain a job with a slightly higher salary, Mr. Li was only able to land such a job in Pennsylvania and was still only making about half of his expected salary at Micheo & Yoon; he therefore lost the benefit of remaining in his home state of New Jersey and experienced a large reduction in expected income. Like the plaintiff in *Pop's Cones*, 704 A.2d at 1322, Mr. Li was unable to enjoy any of the benefit of the promise made by Micheo & Yoon. This stands in contrast to the Sadejs who were able to reap the majority of the benefit from the construction improvements made to their home before they lost the requisite approval. 2019 N.J. Super. Unpub. LEXIS, 1043 at *19.

Under New Jersey law, Mr. Li can likely present a prima facie claim for promissory estoppel. He reasonably relied on Micheo & Yoon's clear and definite promise that he would be employed by them after graduation if he met their conditions and did so to his detriment. Mr. Li satisfied the conditions of the promise and refrained from seeking employment elsewhere in reasonable reliance on Micheo & Yoon's promise; as a result, he was unable to find a big law job and subsequently landed a job that pays a quarter of his expected salary.

CONCLUSION

For all of the foregoing reasons, Appellant Spencer Li respectfully requests that this Court reverse the District Court's Opinion and Order dated September 5, 2023. Respectfully submitted this 13th day of July, 2024.

Dated: July 13, 2024

Respectfully submitted,

Mackenzie Ward/
Chandrasekar & Jackson LLP
New Jersey Bar No. 123456
27 Burr Road
Maplewood, New Jersey
201-123-4567

ATTORNEY FOR APPELLANT

Brief for Appellee

THIS CASE HAS BEEN SCHEDULED FOR ORAL ARGUMENT
March 29–April 2, 2024
No. 20-0028

IN THE UNITED STATES COURT OF APPEALS
FOR THE THIRD CIRCUIT

Spencer Li,
Plaintiff-Appellant,
v.
Micheo & Yoon,
Defendant-Appellee.

APPEAL FROM THE UNITED STATES DISTRICT COURT
FOR THE DISTRICT OF NEW JERSEY

BRIEF FOR APPELLEE

Charli Davis
New Jersey Bar No. 123456
Storey & Henderson LLP
267 Richmond Avenue
South Orange, New Jersey 07079

ATTORNEY FOR APPELLEE

STATEMENT OF JURISDICTION

This case asserts a claim of promissory estoppel pursuant to New Jersey case law. *Malaker Corp. Stockholders Protective Comm. v. First Jersey Nat'l Bank*, 163 N.J. Super. 463 (Super. Ct. App. Div. 1978). The United States Court for the District of New Jersey had subject matter jurisdiction over this matter under 28 U.S.C. § 1332(a) (2018) because the plaintiff is a legal resident of Delaware, the defendant's place of business is in New Jersey, and the amount in controversy is in excess of $75,000. The United States Court of Appeals for the Third Circuit has jurisdiction of this appeal pursuant to 28 U.S.C. § 1291 (2018) because this is an appeal of a final judgment in a civil case. The final order was entered on September 5, 2023, and the notice of appeal was timely filed on October 1, 2023, pursuant to 28 U.S.C. § 2107 (2018).

STATEMENT OF THE ISSUE

Whether Mr. Li can establish he reasonably relied to his detriment on Micheo & Yoon's promise of future employment, even though Micheo & Yoon made a conditional promise two years before its intended performance, Mr. Li did not meet the conditions, and the promise was made during the start of an economic recession, which worsened by the time of performance.

STATEMENT OF THE CASE

Statement of Facts

On February 26, 2023, Spencer Li brought a promissory estoppel claim against his former summer employer, law firm Micheo & Yoon, alleging the firm declined to fulfill its promise of employing him once he graduated law school. R. 1. Micheo & Yoon, a New Jersey-based top 100 law firm, hired Mr. Li during the summer after his first year of law school. R. 21. Initially, Mr. Li exhibited impressive research and analytical skills and a hardworking attitude. *Id.* Because of this, Janet Heinan, Director of Attorney Recruiting, told Mr. Li the firm would extend an offer of full-time employment to him in November of his third year in law school if he maintained a "high G.P.A.," was on journal or moot court, and worked for the firm during the summer after his second year in law school. R. 20.

While law firm culture dictates that the law students who work for a firm during their second-year summer are extended offers of employment, this is only so long as their work product meets requirements. R. 22. Mr. Li did accept an offer from his law school's law review, but elected not to join the editorial staff. R. 12. Similarly, Mr. Li also worked for Micheo & Yoon his second summer with outstanding performance, but decided to "relax" at school and allowed his G.P.A. to drop from a 3.8—at the time Ms. Heinan made the promise—to a 3.5 in his second year, barely above the necessary G.P.A. to remain on the Dean's List, a 3.45. R. 12, 16, 22. Ms. Heinan explained the firm decided to extend Mr. Li the conditional offer of future employment because he was so outstanding his first summer with them. R. 22. However, Ms. Heinan stated the firm typically only offers post-graduate positions to the students in the top 10 to 15 percent of their class, and the firm was disappointed to learn Mr. Li fell well below that—moving from the top 5 percent of his class to only the top one-third. R. 22, 23.

Mr. Li was elated by the potential offer to work with Micheo & Yoon because he wanted to work in his home state of New Jersey and he wished to work in "big law." R. 11. Mr. Li was initially a good candidate for other firms because of his high G.P.A. of 3.8 and his "big law" experience with Micheo & Yoon, but he let his grades fall, and even though there were opportunities for Mr. Li to interview with other firms, he elected not to do so. R. 12, 14, 16.

During the time Ms. Heinan made the promise to extend an offer of employment to Mr. Li nearly two years in the future, there was a moderate economic recession occurring. R. 20. In October of Mr. Li's third year in law school, Ms. Heinan reached out to Mr. Li to explain the firm would no longer be able to hire him due to economic circumstances and the need to reduce the number of the firm's first-year associate offers. R. 17, 24. Marcus Johnson, the Senior Director of Professional Development, Communications, and Research at the American Association of Law Placement, compiles hiring statistics of law firms all over the country. R. 26. Mr. Johnson explained an ongoing economic recession naturally reduces the number of available jobs in the legal field, which can lead to layoffs and reductions in hiring. R. 27. Firms typically only revoke offers in extenuating circumstances, and 35 percent of law firms nationwide actually reported reducing the number of new hires after the recession worsened. *Id.* After Ms. Heinan told Mr. Li Micheo & Yoon would not be able to hire him, he was unable to find a position with another large law firm, but ultimately found employment with a solo practitioner in his hometown of Delaware City, Delaware, that paid him a salary 25 percent of the starting salary at Micheo & Yoon. R. 18. However, Mr. Li currently has a job in Pennsylvania that pays $100,000. R. 11.

Procedural History

On February 26, 2023, Spencer Li filed a Complaint seeking a judgment of $95,000 in the United States District Court for the District of New Jersey claiming that he was entitled to equitable relief by way of promissory estoppel because of Micheo & Yoon's promise to hire him after he graduated law school. R. 1. Micheo & Yoon submitted an answer on March 15, 2023. R. 12. On June 18, 2023, Micheo & Yoon filed a motion for summary judgment and a motion to dismiss Mr. Li's Complaint. R. 15. The United States District Court for the District of New Jersey entered its final judgment on September 5, 2023, granting summary judgment in favor of Micheo & Yoon, and further holding, as a matter of law, that Mr. Li failed to meet his burden of establishing promissory estoppel because while he did incur a detriment, his reliance on the promise of employment was unreasonable. R. 37. Mr. Li entered a notice of appeal to the United States Court of Appeals for the Third Circuit on October 1, 2023. R. 39. On January 3, 2024, the United States Court of Appeals for the Third Circuit certified two issues for appeal: (1) whether Mr. Li reasonably relied on Micheo & Yoon's promise, and (2) whether he in fact shifted his position in detriment on that promise. R. 40.

Standard of Review

On appeal, the standard of review for an issue regarding summary judgment is *de novo*. *In re Ikon Office Solutions, Inc.*, 277 F.3d 658, 665 (3d Cir. 2002). The reviewing court must decide the same question that was before the district court to determine that there were no genuine issues of material fact. Fed. R. Civ. P. 56(c). In applying this review, the court must draw inferences from the evidence in favor of the nonmoving party, without weighing evidence or accessing credibility. *See Abraham v. Raso*, 183 F.3d 279, 287 (3d Cir. 1999).

SUMMARY OF THE ARGUMENT

Not all promises are enforceable; when a promisee fails to meet the conditions associated with the promise, he cannot reasonably expect a court to enforce it. Under New Jersey's application of the promissory estoppel doctrine, there must be clear and convincing evidence to force a promisor to fulfill a promise, limited to when there is no other means to avoid injustice. The plaintiff has the burden to prove all four elements of promissory estoppel in order to prevail: (1) the promisor made a definite promise; (2) the promisor made the promise expecting it to induce reliance by the promisee; (3) the promisee in fact reasonably relied on the promise; and (4) the promisee suffered a definite and substantial detriment because of reliance on the promise. While Janet Heinan did make a promise of conditional employment to the appellant, the United States District Court for the District of New Jersey correctly concluded that the appellant failed to establish a prima facie claim of promissory estoppel because his reliance was not reasonable, nor did he incur a detriment as contemplated by the doctrine.

With regard to reasonable reliance, there must be unambiguous proof the plaintiff relied reasonably on the promise. The conditions attached to the promise, the timing of the promise, and external factors beyond the promisor's control all factor into whether it was reasonable to rely on a promise. In the present case, Mr. Li did not meet the conditions to Micheo & Yoon's promise of future employment because he purposely let his grades fall and, thus, did not meet the condition of a "high G.P.A." Further, the timing of the promise made Mr. Li's reliance unreasonable because the promise could not be fulfilled for almost two years after the promise was made. Finally, there was a moderate economic recession at the time Ms. Heinan made the promise, which only worsened the nearer it got to the time the firm was to fulfill the promise. A recession is clearly out of the control of a law firm and has a negative impact on job hires; this external factor made it unreasonable for Mr. Li to rely on the promise of future employment. For the foregoing reasons, Mr. Li's reliance on Micheo & Yoon's conditional promise of future employment was not reasonable.

Next, the court must determine whether the plaintiff can establish the final element of promissory estoppel—detriment. The plaintiff must show he suffered some substantial hardship or injustice due to reasonable reliance on the promise. There are two essential components to establishing the serious detriment required for promissory estoppel: (1) a definite detriment and (2) a substantial detriment.

A substantial detriment must be more than merely speculative, with some clear way to calculate losses. Mr. Li cannot establish the exact damages he purports to have suffered because Mr. Li had no past earnings and did not forgo current employment, so he did not give up any definite salary to work with Micheo & Yoon. In fact, Mr. Li obtained some benefit by working with a large law firm, gaining valuable work experience.

To maintain there was a substantial detriment, the plaintiff must show he lost all or most of the benefit of the promise. Mr. Li did not suffer a substantial detriment because Mr. Li was not prevented from seeking opportunities with other law firms. Actually, Mr. Li forwent the opportunity to interview with other law firms. As Mr. Li gained a benefit from working with Micheo & Yoon, and there would be no way to determine if he could have gotten a similar job if he had attempted to, Mr. Li did not suffer a substantial detriment.

There is no viable claim of promissory estoppel in this case because Mr. Li neither relied reasonably on Micheo & Yoon's conditional promise of employment, nor did he actually suffer a definite and substantial detriment. Promissory estoppel is a serious remedy reserved for those who have experienced substantial hardship and loss, not for plaintiffs who have failed to meet specific conditions of a promise, ignored surrounding circumstances, and actually obtained a benefit from their reliance—such as is the situation in the present case.

ARGUMENT AND CITATIONS OF AUTHORITIES

I. Mr. Li's reliance on Micheo & Yoon's promise of future employment was unreasonable and Mr. Li did not suffer a definite and substantial detriment; accordingly the United States District Court for the District of New Jersey correctly held Mr. Li failed to establish a prima facie claim of promissory estoppel.

"The intention of a party with regard to his future acts is not the foundation upon which an estoppel may be built." *In re Phillips Petroleum Sec. Litig.*, 881 F.2d 1236, 1250 (3d Cir. 1989) (quoting *Metro. Life Ins. Co. v. Childs Co.*, 130 N.E. 295 (N.Y. 1921)). Promissory estoppel is a remedy by which a promisee may seek redress when a promisor should reasonably expect his promise to induce forbearance or action on the part of the promisee, limited to when injustice can only be avoided by the enforcement of the promise. Restatement (Second) of Contracts § 139(1) (Am. Law Inst. 1981). Promissory estoppel is applicable to *in futuro* promises where the promisor intends to abandon the promise, or where the promise is intended to influence another into action or forbearance of a legal right. *See Friedman v. Tappan Dev. Corp.*, 126 A.2d

646, 653 (N.J. 1956). Promissory estoppel "cannot be established by mere proof that a sophisticated individual made a decision based on his own business judgment, rather than relied on an express promise by the promisor." *Johnson v. Dunkin' Donuts Franchising L.L.C.*, Civil Action No. 11-1117, 2014 U.S. Dist. LEXIS 88446 at *1, *42 (W.D. Pa. June 30, 2014) (affirmed by *Derrick v. Dunkin' Donuts Franchising, L.L.C.*, 610 F. App'x 208 (3d Cir. 2015)).

This Court has affirmed the four-part test set out by the New Jersey courts when evaluating whether a claim of promissory estoppel is valid: (1) the promisor made a definite promise; (2) the promisor made the promise expecting it to induce reliance by the promisee; (3) the promisee in fact reasonably relied on the promise; and (4) the promisee suffered a definite and substantial detriment because of reliance on the promise. *Schley v. Microsoft Corp.*, No. 08-3589 (DRD), 2008 U.S. Dist. LEXIS 96059, at *1 (D.N.J. Nov. 24, 2008) (citing *Pop's Cones, Inc. v. Resorts Intern. Hotel, Inc.*, 307 N.J. Super. 461, 469, 704 A.2d 1321 (N.J.Super. A.D. 1998)). The plaintiff has the burden to prove all four elements. *In re Phillips*, 881 F.2d at 1250. Promissory estoppel requires clear and convincing evidence to compel individuals to fulfill a promise. *Johnson*, 2014 U.S. Dist. LEXIS 88446 at *42 (affirmed by *Derrick*, 610 F. App'x at 208). While Janet Heinan likely made a promise to Mr. Li with the expectation it could induce reliance, Mr. Li cannot establish the other two elements necessary for a viable promissory estoppel claim.

Because Mr. Li was not reasonable in his reliance and he suffered no definite and substantial detriment, this Court should affirm the holding of summary judgment in favor of Micheo & Yoon.

A. **Mr. Li's reliance on Micheo & Yoon's statement was unreasonable because he failed to meet the conditions of that statement, there was an extended length of time from when Micheo & Yoon made the promise to when it would have fulfilled it, and there were uncontrollable, external forces that made reliance on that statement unreasonable.**

To satisfy the third element of promissory estoppel, a plaintiff must provide unambiguous proof his reliance was reasonable. *Johnson*, U.S. District LEXIS 88446 at *42 (affirmed in *Derrick*, 610 F. App'x at 208). The plaintiff must show that he reasonably relied on a representation made by the defendant, which induced him to abandon an existing right or influenced him to act or refrain from acting. *Friedman*, 126 A.2d at 653. When determining whether reliance on a promise is reasonable in a promissory estoppel claim, this Court as well as New Jersey courts look to several factors, including: the immediate circumstances surrounding the promise, the language of the promise, and external factors that could affect the reliability of the promise. *See In re Phillips*, 881 F.2d at 1250 (holding the expression of intention regarding future acts does not induce a reasonable reliance); *see also Landan v. Wal-Mart Real Estate Bus. Tr.*, No. 2:12cv926, 2016 U.S. Dist. LEXIS 129481, at *1 (W.D. Pa. Sep. 22, 2016) (affirmed by *Landan v. Wal-Mart Real Estate Bus. Tr.*, 775 F. App'x 39 (3d Cir. 2019)) (holding the "mere expression of future intention" cannot be reasonable); *see also Thomas v. Princeton Univ.*, No. A-0680-14T1, 2016 N.J. Super. LEXIS 2515, at *1 (Super. Ct. App. Div. Nov. 23, 2016) (holding a temporary employee's reliance on a promise of permanent employment was unreasonable, especially considering the promise was made two years in the past); *see also Massaro Ltd. P'ship (Park W. Two) v. Baker & Taylor Inc.*, 161 F. App'x 185 (3d Cir. 2005) (holding that it was not reasonable to rely on a promise when specific conditions of the promise were not met); *see also E. Orange Bd. of Educ. v. N.J. Sch. Const. Corp.*, 963 A.2d 865 (N.J. Super. Ct. App. Div. 2009) (holding negative, external economic impacts can make it unreasonable to rely on a promise).

It is not reasonable to rely on a promise when the promisee has not met the conditions of the promise. *Bonczek v. Carter-Wallace, Inc.*, 701 A.2d 742, 744–46 (N.J. Super. Ct. App. Div. 1997) (holding where the plaintiff did not meet the condition of positive reference checks, it was not reasonable for him to rely on a promise of employment); *Massaro*, 161 F. App'x at 186. For example, in *Massaro*, a partnership's claims arose out of a letter of intent (LOI), pursuant to which the corporation agreed to rent property to the partnership. 161 F. App'x at 186. The corporation's performance was specifically conditioned upon the corporation's board approving the rental decision, which ended up being denied. *Id.* Because the specific condition of approval was not met, the court held it was not reasonable to rely on the promise in the LOI. *Id.* Conversely, when the promisee has met all the necessary conditions, reliance is reasonable. *Royal Assocs. v. Concannon*, 490 A.2d 357, 357 (N.J. Super. Ct. App. Div. 1985) (holding tenants relied reasonably on a landlord's promise to let them keep their dog despite the no pets policy because they complied with all of the landlord's conditions); *Wiegand v. Motiva Enters., LLC*, 295 F. Supp. 2d 465 (D.N.J. 2003). In *Wiegand*, the plaintiff disseminated racist music on his public platform. 295 F. Supp. 2d at 466. The plaintiff asserted his employer promised he could remain employed if he met certain conditions to ensure that his web-based business was not further connected to the defendants. *Id.* at 469. Because the plaintiff met all the conditions, the court held a reasonable fact finder could find his reliance was reasonable. *Id.* at 479.

Reliance on a promise becomes less reasonable when the performance due is remote in time because it is unreasonable to believe the promise will come to fruition in such uncertain conditions. *See In re Phillips*, 881 F.2d at 1250 (holding a promise of future intent does not give rise to reasonable reliance); *see also Thomas v. Princeton Univ.*, No. A-0680-14T1, 2016 N.J. Super. LEXIS 2515, at *1 (Super. Ct. App. Div. Nov. 23, 2016) (holding a term employee was not reasonable in relying on a promise of permanent employment due to his temporary status and because the promise was made two years prior to when he was fired); *see also E. Orange Bd. of Educ. v. N.J. Sch. Const. Corp.*, 963 A.2d 865 (N.J. Super. Ct. App. Div. 2009) (holding it was not reasonable for a school board to rely on state funds for school construction projects in the midst of statewide budget cuts). For example, in *Thomas*, a term employee was promised a permanent position with his employer once his current construction project was complete. 2016 N.J. Super. LEXIS 2515, at *1. These promises continued for two years while the employee continued his project and passed up opportunities to apply for permanent positions. *Id.* The court held it would not be reasonable to rely on the employer's promises given the conditions surrounding the promise—namely the employee's term status and the elapsed time from the date of the original promise. *Id.*

Where the promise should mature within a practical timeframe, reliance may be reasonable. *Schley*, 2008 U.S. Dist. LEXIS 96059 at *17; *Goldfarb v. Solimine*, No. A-3740-16T2, 2019 N.J. Super. LEXIS 1472, at *1, *6–7 (Super. Ct. App. Div. June 26, 2019) (holding it was reasonable to rely on a promise where the plaintiff's employment was to begin immediately and the defendant promised to memorialize the agreement in writing). For instance, in *Schley*, the plaintiff received a written employment offer, engaged in extensive negotiations over compensation and benefits, signed the final offer, and the defendant encouraged him to purchase a new home and quit his job. U.S. Dist. LEXIS 96059 at *3–4. This Court held it was reasonable for the plaintiff to rely on the promise since he had signed the employment offer and was encouraged to move immediately. *Id.* at *17.

A downturn in economic circumstances can negatively impact the reasonableness of relying on a promise. *See E. Orange*, 963 A.2d at 874–75; *see also Thomas*, 2016 N.J. Super. LEXIS 2515 at *9. For instance, in *E. Orange*, a school board sought to compel New Jersey Schools Construction Corporation (SCC) to proceed with certain school construction projects that were delayed because of statewide budget cuts. 963 A.2d at 866–67. The SCC was responsible for distributing the funds for similar projects at public schools around the state. *Id.* at 867. Prior to the suit, the SCC determined it would not be able to fund all of the projects due to a lack of funds. *Id.* Even though the school board previously received approval for their projects and was on the original priority list, its projects were cut in the reprioritization. *Id.* at 870. The court held it was not reasonable for the school board to rely on the approval of their proposed projects given no specific project was approved, especially in light of the dire funding issue. *Id.* Similarly, in *Thomas*, budget cuts at a university prevented it from hiring a term construction employee as permanent even after promising to do so. 2016 N.J. Super. LEXIS 2515 at *3–4. Because of the budgetary cutbacks the university had fewer projects available, which meant there was not enough revenue to pay employees. *Id.* at *6. Because the university had legitimate business reasons to forgo hiring the term employee—specifically budget cutbacks—the court held it was not reasonable for the employee to rely on the university's promise made before the cutbacks. *Id.* at *9.

However, when the surrounding circumstances are within the control of the promisor, the court has held it was reasonable to rely on the promise. *Pop's Cones, Inc. v. Resorts Intern. Hotel, Inc.*, 704 A.2d 1321, 1330 (N.J. Super. Ct. App. Div. 1998); *see also Peck v. Imedia, Inc.*, 679 A.2d 745, 747 (N.J. Super. Ct. App. Div. 1996) (holding that an employee reasonably relied on an oral offer for a full-time position that was subsequently rescinded because the decision was based only on the employer's change of mind about the employee's fit). In *Pop's Cones*, a casino induced a store owner to give up her lease at her current location to relocate to the casino. 704 A.2d at 1326. The store owner repeatedly told the casino when she needed to renew her current lease. *Id.* at 1322. The casino told the store owner not to renew her lease and to "pack up ... and plan on moving." *Id.* Because virtually nothing remained to be determined by the parties, the casino told the store owner to "pack up," and it was at the casino's sole discretion to back out of the promise, the court held there was a claim of promissory estoppel because it was reasonable for the store owner to rely on the promise. *Id.* at 1326.

Mr. Li's reliance on the promise of future employment was not reasonable because he did not meet all of the conditions of the promise. Ms. Heinan specifically told Mr. Li he had to keep up a "high G.P.A." in order to receive an offer in his last year of law school. R. 20. Mr. Li had a G.P.A. of 3.8 at the time Ms. Heinan made the promise, but he purposefully decided to "relax" his work ethic and allowed his G.P.A to drop to a 3.5. R. 12, 16. When the promisee does not meet the conditions of the promise, the court is unlikely to hold that reliance on the promise is reasonable. *Massaro*, 161 F. App'x at 186. Like in *Massaro, id.*, where the deal was conditioned on receiving board approval, Mr. Li's employment was conditioned on a high G.P.A. R. 20. While Mr. Li's G.P.A. of 3.5 is slightly above the necessary G.P.A. required to make the Dean's List, a 3.45, Ms. Heinan explained Micheo & Yoon typically only takes students in the top 10 to 15 percent of their class. R. 16, 22. This is clearly distinguishable from cases where the plaintiff was found to have reasonably relied on a promise because he met all of the conditions because Mr. Li did not meet the condition of maintaining a "high G.P.A." In *Wiegand*, the plaintiff met all the conditions set forth by his employer, so the court found he could have reasonably relied on the promise of continued employment. 295 F. Supp. 2d at 469, 479. One of the reasons Micheo & Yoon hired Mr. Li was because of his hardworking attitude, but Ms. Heinan expressed that the firm was disappointed Mr. Li fell from the top 5 percent of his class to only the top third. R. 21, 23. Therefore, because Micheo & Yoon could have made a practical decision in determining Mr. Li did not meet the conditions of its promise, it was not reasonable for Mr. Li to rely on the promise.

Mr. Li not only failed to meet the conditions of the law firm's promise, but the timing of the promise made it so that no reasonable person should have relied on it. It was not reasonable for Mr. Li to rely on Micheo & Yoon's promise of employment because the promise was made too distant in time from when it was to be fulfilled. Janet Heinan, the Director of Attorney Recruiting for Micheo & Yoon, made the promise to employ Mr. Li almost two years before Mr. Li would be able to take the position. R. 20. In *Thomas*, the court held a term employee who relied on his employer's promise to become a permanent employee two years before being terminated did not rely reasonably because the promise was too far removed from the date of maturation. 2016 N.J. Super. LEXIS 2515 at *10. Like the temporary nature of the term employee, *id.*, Mr. Li was a summer associate at the time of the law firm's promise, meaning he was only a temporary employee. R. 21. Unlike situations where the courts have found plaintiffs were reasonable in relying on a promise of immediate employment, *Schley*, 2008 U.S. Dist. LEXIS 96059 at *17, Mr. Li was also promised employment for a remote time in the future. The plaintiff in *Schley* was also promised employment, but he was found to have relied reasonably because he entered into extensive negotiations, signed a final offer, and was encouraged to move immediately after the negotiations were completed. *Id.* In contrast, Mr. Li was not supposed to start until two years later and never signed any written offer. R. 20.

The external economic forces that affected the law firm's ability to deliver on its promise made it unreasonable for Mr. Li to rely on the promise of employment. At the time Ms. Heinan made her statements of possible future employment to Mr. Li, there was a moderate economic recession. R. 20. When Ms. Heinan informed Mr. Li the firm would no longer be able to employ him, many firms were also experiencing a decrease in job availability due to the dip in the economy. R. 24, 26. According to Marcus Johnson, the Senior Director of Professional Development, Communications, and Research at the American Association of Law Placement, who compiles hiring statistics of law firms all over the country, 35 percent of law firms nationwide had to reduce the number of new hires after the recession worsened. R. 26, 27. In *E. Orange*, statewide funding cuts led to the SCC defunding certain school projects. 963 A.2d at 874–75. In light of the dire funding issues for school projects across the state, it was not reasonable for the school's board to rely on promises it would receive funding for their projects. *Id.* at 870. Similarly, Micheo & Yoon likely was affected by the negative effects a recession can have on businesses nationwide. Ms. Heinan told Mr. Li the firm would be unable to hire him due to economic circumstances. R. 24. In *Thomas*, the court held when there are viable business reasons for not hiring someone and budgetary cutbacks, it is not reasonable to rely on a promise of employment. 2016 N.J. Super. LEXIS 2515 at *9. The employer in

Thomas had no new construction projects that would supply it with funds to hire new permanent employees. *Id.* at *4. Mr. Johnson explained that an ongoing economic recession naturally reduces the number of available jobs in the legal field. R. 27. In the context of a slowing economy, which was evident at the time Ms. Heinan made the promise to Mr. Li, R. 20, it would not be reasonable to rely on such promises. Unlike the defendant in *Pop's Cones*, 704 A.2d at 1326, who was in complete control of the circumstances surrounding its promise, and in fact encouraged the plaintiff to continue to rely on its promises, an economic recession is not in the control of a law firm and no one at the law firm explicitly continued to encouraged Mr. Li to stay with the firm.

It was not reasonable for Mr. Li to rely on Micheo & Yoon's promise of future employment because Mr. Li did not meet the conditions of the promise, was offered employment two years before he could take the position, and there were negative economic factors beyond the law firm's control impacting its ability to hire Mr. Li.

B. **Mr. Li did not incur a detriment in reliance on Micheo & Yoon's promise because the detriment was too speculative, and in fact Mr. Li received a benefit from working with the law firm.**

The last essential element of a promissory estoppel claim is proving the promisee suffered some detriment in reliance on the promise. *Ankerstjerne v. Schlumberger Ltd.*, No. 03-3607, 2004 U.S. Dist. LEXIS 9927 at *1 (E.D. Pa. 2004) (citing *Jayne v. Archdiocese of Phila.*, No. 93-4039, 1994 U.S. Dist. LEXIS 3810 at *3–4 (E.D. Pa. Mar. 25, 1994)) (affirmed by *Ankerstjerne v. Schlumberger, Ltd.*, 155 F. App'x 48 (3d Cir. 2005)). In this Court and the New Jersey courts, there are two essential components that must be present to establish the element of detrimental reliance: (1) a definite detriment and (2) a substantial detriment. *Id.* (holding there must be forbearance of a definite and substantial nature); *Malaker*, 395 A.2d at 232 (holding a detriment must be substantial in nature); *Sadej v. Arturi*, No. A-1424-16T1, 2019 N.J. Super. LEXIS 1043 at *1, *22 (Super. Ct. App. Div. May 7, 2019) (holding a detriment must be definite and substantial); *Toll Bros., Inc. v. Bd. of Chosen Freeholders of Burlington*, 944 A.2d at *1, *19 (N.J. 2008) (holding there must be definite and substantial detriment for a viable promissory estoppel claim).

Definite detriment requires the damages the promisee purports to have suffered to be more than merely speculative. *Ankerstjerne*, 2004 U.S. Dist. LEXIS 9927 at *1 (E.D. Pa. 2004) (citing *Jayne*, 1994 U.S. Dist.

LEXIS 3810 at *3–4) (affirmed by *Schlumberger, Ltd.*, 155 F. App'x at 51); *Village Square Madison Ave., LLC v. TD Bank*, N.A., 2016 N.J. Super. LEXIS 269 at *24. For example, in *Village Square*, the defendant pulled out of an agreement to obtain zoning and develop a property with Village Square, causing Village Square to incur costs in reliance on developing the area. 2016 N.J. Super. LEXIS 269 at *19–20. The plaintiff failed to show that the defendant was not diligent in pursuing the agreement because the defendant spent two years attempting to obtain zoning approval and it became clear it would not be able to obtain approval. *Id.* at *22. The court held that Village Square's assertions it could have reaped financial gain from the sale of the property had it not relied on the defendant's promises to work together were too speculative to constitute a definite detriment. *Id.* at *24.

Only where the promisee can show there is a clear way to calculate lost earnings and he suffered some external, additional cost as a result of relying on a promise have New Jersey courts allowed recovery. *Swider v. Ha-Lo Indus.*, 134 F. Supp. 2d 607 (D.N.J. 2001) (holding the plaintiff needs to have undergone some external, additional costs in reliance on the defendant's representations); *Goldfarb*, 2019 N.J. Super. LEXIS 1472 at *1, *29–30 (Super. Ct. App. Div. June 26, 2019). In *Goldfarb*, the plaintiff was promised employment with the defendant to handle the defendant's assets. 2019 N.J. Super. LEXIS 1472 at *1. In reliance on the defendant's promises, the plaintiff quit his current job, but the defendant withdrew the offer before the plaintiff could start. *Id.* The plaintiff was able to prove what his salary was for several years prior to quitting his job, and showed that once he found a new job it was much less than he made previously and what he was promised by the defendant. *Id.* at *2, *26. Because the plaintiff was able to point to specific financial losses based on his changed employment in reliance on the defendant's promise, the court held there was a definite detriment that would allow a promissory estoppel claim. *Id.* at *30.

This Court has refused to recognize damages for "roads not taken." *Ankerstjerne*, 2004 U.S. Dist. LEXIS 9927 at *1 (E.D. Pa. 2004) (citing *Jayne*, 1994 U.S. Dist. LEXIS 3810 at *3–4) (affirmed by *Schlumberger, Ltd.*, 155 F. App'x at 51). The non-exercise of a right to seek opportunity elsewhere is not a substantial detriment such that one may prevail on a claim of detrimental reliance. *See Malaker*, 395 A.2d at 232 (holding the forbearance from seeking funding from other sources in reliance on the bank's promise to supply a loan was not sufficiently substantial to show detriment); *see also Friedman*, 126 A.2d at 652 (holding where the plaintiff held land to be sold at a special price to a buyer, but the buyer later backed out, there was no detriment because the seller expended nothing and could still sell to someone else). For example, this Court has noted that "[c]ourts have found that refraining from pursuing other employment opportunities altogether is not a sufficient detriment to support a promissory estoppel claim." *Ankerstjerne*, 2004 U.S. Dist. LEXIS 9927 at *1 (E.D. Pa. 2004) (affirmed by *Schlumberger*, 155 F. App'x at 51). In *Schlumberger*, the plaintiff worked for the defendant for a year on a one-year contract, but continued working past that term. 155 F. App'x at 50. He claimed he detrimentally relied on his employer's promises that he should still receive bonuses at the same rates he did during his year contract. *Id.* However, the court held there was no evidence indicating the plaintiff took a substantial change in position on this reliance because he did not show he had to forgo taking other projects with better bonuses or that he had to refuse other positions. *Id.* at 51.

Moreover, where the promisee receives most of the benefits of a promise, there is likely no substantial detriment. *Pane v. RCA Corp.*, 868 F.2d 631 (3d Cir. 1989); *Sadej*, 2019 N.J. Super. LEXIS 1043 at *22. For instance, in *Pane*, a company, RCA, was about to merge with GE, and in doing so decided to induce certain employees to remain with the company by giving them an attractive severance agreement. 868 F.2d at 633. The plaintiff was on the list of employees to receive this offer, but did not get a copy of the agreement. *Id.* Later, he received a memo addressed to "Limited Severance Plan Participants" stating he could exercise his option to purchase RCA stocks to increase the value of severance payments. *Id.* at 634. The plaintiff claimed this induced action on his part, and the anxiety of purchasing stock was a detriment. *Id.* at 638. However, the court held the plaintiff still received the benefit of the agreement because he could sell his stocks for a profit, and alleviate any anxiety connected to owning the stock that way. *Id.* It did not matter that RCA got the benefit of his continued employment because promissory estoppel is about detriment to the promisee, not benefit to the promisor. *Id.* Similarly, the plaintiffs in *Sadej* received zoning permits to make improvements to their home. 2019 N.J. Super. Unpub. LEXIS 1043 at *2. When they completed about 80 percent of the work, the city issued a stop order, saying the improvements did not comply with the permits.

Id. The couple still completed most of the improvements (except for attaching their detached garage), was only held up for seven days, and got income from renting out the property. *Id.* at 23–24. Because of the minimal delay and the majority of projects were still completed, the court determined there was no substantial detriment. *Id.*

Where a promisee is prevented from obtaining all or most of the benefit of a promise, then the court is likely to find a substantial detriment. *See Onorato Const., Inc. v. Eastman Const. Co.*, 711 A.2d 1363 (N.J. Super. Ct. App. Div. 1998); *see also King James Care Ctr. of Chatham 415 S. Blvd. Chatham v. Richardson*, 2018 N.J. Super. LEXIS 4394 at *25–26 (holding where the daughter of a nursing home resident neglected to pay any of the outstanding balance, there was a substantial detriment). For example, in *Onorato*, a general contractor was told by its subcontractor and the plaintiff that the subcontractor was in financial difficulties and the general contractor should either pay the plaintiff directly or issue a joint check. 711 A.2d at 1364. The general contractor acknowledged it would do so, sent a portion of the payment as a joint check, but then later sent the rest to the subcontractor alone, who was insolvent. *Id.* Because the general contractor knew of the issues, acknowledged them orally and in writing, yet issued only one check as a joint payment, the court held there was a substantial detriment. *Id.* at 1365–66. Likewise, when the promisee has no other option but to rely on the promisee's assertions, the court may find a substantial detriment. *King James*, 2018 N.J. Super. LEXIS 4394 at *25–26. In *King James*, the daughter of a patient in a nursing home explicitly asserted she was not personally liable for her mother's payments to the nursing home. *Id.* at * 3. However, she had power of attorney over her mother and previously assured the nursing home that she would "promptly" fill out the necessary Medicaid paperwork, and would pay for the remaining balance of her mother's care from her mother's assets. *Id.* at *3, *5. The court held because the daughter allowed two years of payments to accrue while assuring the nursing home she would be responsible for the payments if Medicaid did not pay them, the nursing home incurred a substantial detriment for which the daughter was responsible. *Id.* at *25–26.

Mr. Li cannot establish he suffered a definite detriment as a result of Micheo & Yoon's promise because his alleged damages are speculative, as there is no way to calculate the exact damages Mr. Li incurred. Mr. Li may have been a good candidate early in his law school career because of his high G.P.A. and "big law" experience, but he later let his grades drop and ranking fall by over 25 percent. R. 12, 16, 23. The alleged detriment in this case is similar to that in *Village Square*, where the plaintiff could not establish it could have achieved financial gain if it took an alternate route from working with the defendant because there was no way to establish what Village Square could have made if it did not work with the defendant. 2016 N.J. Super. LEXIS 269 at *24. Analogously, Mr. Li did not apply to any other law firm positions, R. 14, so there is no way to prove he could have acquired a legal job of the same caliber and salary as Micheo & Yoon had he never relied on Ms. Heinan's promise and worked for the law firm over his second summer. In contrast, where there is a clear way to calculate lost earnings, the courts have found a definite detriment. *Goldfarb*, 2019 N.J. Super. LEXIS 1472 at *1. In *Goldfarb*, the plaintiff used past earnings to establish a definite loss when he quit his job in reliance on the defendant's promise of employment. *Id.* However, unlike in *Goldfarb*, *id.* at *30, where the plaintiff could point to specific loss, Mr. Li had no past earnings and did not forgo current employment, so he did not give up a definite salary to work with Micheo & Yoon.

Just as there is no definite detriment, Mr. Li also did not suffer a substantial detriment because Mr. Li was not prevented from seeking opportunities with other law firms. While Mr. Li was told he would receive an offer if he continued to work with Micheo & Yoon, the law firm never dissuaded Mr. Li from applying to other firms. R. 14. Indeed, Mr. Li himself elected not to interview with other firms. Using forgone potential opportunities as the way to establish detrimental reliance is too speculative to establish a substantial detriment. For instance, in *Schlumberger*, the defendant allegedly made an oral promise to pay the plaintiff bonuses at the same rates he was paid in previous years where he had a contract, but then did not pay the plaintiff at that rate. 155 F. App'x at 50, 51. This Court held forgoing alternative job prospects in reliance on the defendant's promise was too speculative to be substantial. *Id.* at 51. Similarly, Mr. Li declined the chance to seek out alternative employment. R. 14. There would be no way to determine if Mr. Li would have received another job offer from a top law firm, or what salary he would have earned at another firm.

In fact, that Mr. Li obtained a benefit from the experience of working at a prestigious law firm like Micheo & Yoon minimizes his claim of substantial detriment. Mr. Li was able to stay in his home state while working with Micheo & Yoon and the firm was diligent in giving Mr. Li "big law" experience. R. 11, 12. Mr. Li's experience strengthened his marketability and may have contributed to his ability to find a job in an uncertain job market. Just as in *Pane*, 868 F.2d at 638, where the plaintiff received a comparable benefit with the option to sell his stocks for a profit, Mr. Li obtained a comparable benefit in experience. In *Sadej*, the court held that because the promisee received most of the value of the promise, there was no substantial detriment. 2019 N.J. Super. LEXIS 1043 at *23–*24. Here, the value Mr. Li received in continuing to work for Micheo & Yoon outweighed any detriment he may have incurred in relying on its promise of post-graduation employment.

While Mr. Li's salary with a solo practitioner in Delaware is seventy-five percent less than the starting salary at Micheo & Yoon, R. 18, the cost of housing in the largest city in Delaware is 73 percent less than in New Jersey. *2020 Cost of Living Calculator: Jersey City, New Jersey vs Wilmington, Delaware* (2020), https://www.bestplaces.net/cost-of-living/jersey-city-nj/wilmington-de/110000 (last visited July 7, 2020). Moreover, Mr. Li is currently making over half of what he would have made with Micheo & Yoon at his job in Pennsylvania, R. 11, and the cost of living in Pennsylvania is almost half of what it is in New Jersey. *2020 Cost of Living Calculator: Philadelphia, Pennsylvania vs Jersey City, New Jersey* (2020), https://www.bestplaces.net/cost-of-living/philadelphia-pa/jersey-city-nj/100000 (last visited July 7, 2020). This is distinguishable from cases where the court has found a substantial detriment when the plaintiff is prevented from obtaining most of the benefit of a promise, or is in complete reliance on the promisor. *Onorato*, 711 A.2d at 1364; *King James*, 2018 N.J. Super. LEXIS 4394 at *3, *5. In *Onorato*, the promisor acknowledged the promise in writing, yet still prevented the subcontractor from being paid. 711 A.2d at 1364, 1365–66. Here, however, Micheo & Yoon never promised Mr. Li a specific salary, and still gave him "big law" experience. R. 12, 20. Unlike in *King James*, 2018 N.J. Super. LEXIS 4394 at *3, *5, where the daughter repeatedly assured the nursing home she would take care of her mother's nursing home payments and allowed two years of costs to accrue, Mr. Li did not amass any debt and Micheo & Yoon did not continuously and explicitly assure Mr. Li of future payment. Given the cost-of-living differences, Mr. Li did not lose a substantial salary compared to that which he would have earned at Micheo & Yoon.

Mr. Li cannot establish that Micheo & Yoon's broken promise of future employment incurred definite or substantial detriment because Mr. Li did not lose any assured income, it would be too speculative to calculate potential lost earnings, Micheo & Yoon did not prevent Mr. Li from seeking alternative employment opportunities at any time, and Mr. Li's earnings at his subsequent places of employment are relatively comparable.

CONCLUSION

For all the foregoing reasons, Appellee Micheo & Yoon requests that this Court affirm the District Court's Opinion and Order dated September 5, 2023.

Index